How to Sound Really Clever

600 Words You Need to Know

By Hubert van den Bergh

Bloomsbury Information
An imprint of Bloomsbury Publishing Plc

B L O O M S B U R Y
LONDON · OXFORD · NEW YORK · NEW DELHI · SYDNEY

Bloomsbury Information

An imprint of Bloomsbury Publishing Plc

50 Bedford Square	1385 Broadway
London	New York
WC1B 3DP	NY 10018
UK	USA

www.bloomsbury.com

BLOOMSBURY and the Diana logo are trademarks of Bloomsbury Publishing Plc

First published 2013
This hardback edition published 2017

© Hubert van den Bergh, 2013, 2016
Copyright illustrations © Sandra Howgate, 2013 and 2016

Hubert van den Bergh has asserted his right under the Copyright, Designs and
Patents Act, 1988, to be identified as Author of this work.

British Library Cataloguing-in-Publication Data
A catalogue record for this book is available from the British Library.

ISBN: HB: 978-1-4729-5460-2

Library of Congress Cataloging-in-Publication Data
A catalog record for this book is available from the Library of Congress.

Design by Fiona Pike, Pike Design, Winchester
Typeset by Saxon Graphics Ltd, Derby
Printed and bound in Great Britain

To my parents, John and Marion, and 10 siblings:
Antonia, James, Mary, John,
George, Elizabeth, Benedict,
Caroline, Sarah Jane and Lucy.

Introduction

Boris Johnson: what a fun man. And the reason? His joyful approach to language. To Boris's mind, the ending of the Olympics was a 'final, tear-sodden juddering climax'; and the female beach volleyball contestants were 'glistening like wet otters'. As well as this salacious turn of phrase, Boris has a penchant for slightly tricky words that brighten up everyone's day – just look at these three examples:

On the Olympic Village: 'Tessa Jowell...takes her duties as deputy mayor of the village so seriously that she actually **pernoctates** in the village, sharing the life of the young men and women on whom we pin our hopes.' *(The Daily Telegraph)*

On Roger Federer: '...money is surely among the **embrocations** that has kept his genius so elastic for so long.' *(The Daily Telegraph)*

On Norway's mass killer, Anders Breivik: 'Some people will read his dismal **expectorations** and conclude that this inflammatory guff is what really drove him on.' *(The Daily Telegraph)*

But what do the three words in bold mean? Read this book if you want to find out. All three are in here, along with another 600 or so that are equally fun (whilst still managing to be common currency, and definitely not 'dead' or obsolete). For the last two years, I've been jotting down the most wonderful words I've come across (in conversations and in newspaper articles), and this book is the result. These are the words that made me raise an admiring eyebrow, when I heard them trip off other people's tongues; and smile at, when I came across them in newsprint.

As you read them, some will give you that delightful rush as you recognise *le mot juste* – like **iridescent** (to describe the rainbow sheen of the soap bubbles in your bath), **umami** (of that meat-like taste in mushrooms and miso soup) and **casuistry** (of an argument that sounds great at the time, but afterwards doesn't quite add up).

And also the stories behind everyday words which pepper this book will surprise you – like that behind **pastiche** (and why it derives from the Italian for 'piecrust'); **piece of cake** (and what it

1

How to Sound Really Clever

has to do with American slaves working in 1900); and **virago** (an insult that started out as a compliment – to Joan of Arc).

Finally, you'll be able to clear up those linguistic riddles that no one around a dinner table ever seems to be able to – such as the true meanings of the words **nonplussed** (which people use – wrongly – to mean 'not bothered'), **disinterested** (which everyone thinks means 'not interested', but actually is all about money) and **gauntlet** (which in fact boasts two completely separate meanings and backstories, both steeped in buckets of blood: but how to tell which from which?).

Perfect for reading for 10 minutes before drifting into the arms of **Morpheus**, you'll amuse yourself – as well as any **interlocutor** (who'll be relishing your richer vocabulary) – with the answers in this book, and also ensuring your diction approaches the level of that most cunning linguist of all, Boris himself.

PS If a word's pronunciation is difficult, I have included a phonetic guide to saying it out loud; if it's not, I haven't.

'For a moment she rediscovered the purpose of her life. She was here on earth to grasp the meaning of its wild enchantment and to call each thing by its right name...'

Boris Pasternak, *Doctor Zhivago*

(in) abeyance (noun) = **to be temporarily unused** (*pronounced 'uh-bey-uhns'*) from the Old French *abeance*: aspiration to a title, from *a*: toward + *beer*: to gape

e.g. Her hair was unkempt and her appearance slovenly: from this, he deduced her love-life was **in abeyance**

abject (adj.) = *(of a situation)* **very degrading; *(of a person)* very degraded** from the Latin *abjectus*, past participle of *abjicere*: to reject, from *ab-*: away, and *jacere*: to throw

e.g. One art critic has described Tracy Emin's condom-filled tent as '**abject**'

to abjure (verb) = **to renounce in a solemn way** (*pronounced 'ab-jur'*) from the Latin *abjurare*, from *ab-*: away, and *jurare*: to swear

e.g. *Harry Potter* star Daniel Radcliffe has said of his drinking, 'As much as I would love to be a person that goes to parties and has a couple of drinks and has a nice time, that doesn't work for me. I do that very unsuccessfully'; consequently, the star has now **abjured** alcohol

abnegation (noun) = **saying 'no' to something desired** from the Latin *abnegare*, from *ab-*: away, and *negare*: to deny

e.g. The late Christopher Hitchens – who was a militant atheist – once described religious belief as 'limitless **abnegation**...of self: a celestial North Korea'

abrasion (noun) = **the process of gradually wearing away** from the Latin *abradere*, from *ab-*: away, and *radere*: to scrape

e.g. He spent too much time at work, and the resulting **abrasions** in their relationship caused them to divorce

abrogate (verb) = *(of an agreement)* **to reject** (*pronounced 'ab-ruh-geyt'*) from the Latin, *abrogare*: to repeal, from *ab-*: away, and *rogare*: to propose a law

e.g. Critics of Bill Clinton said that, as a result of his behaviour with Monica Lewinsky, he had **abrogated** his marital responsibilities

5

acedia (noun) = **unaccountable melancholy** (*pronounced 'a-see-dee-a'*) from the Greek, *akedia*: indifference, from *a-*:without, and *kedos*: care

e.g. Halfway through my boss's motivational speech, my mind began to wander, and soon **acedia** took a grip of me

to acquiesce (verb) = **to accept something with reluctance but without protesting** (*pronounced 'ak-wee-es'*) from the Latin, *acquiescere*, from *ad-*: to + *quiescere*: to rest

e.g. When he was 25, Ayrton Senna dated 15-year-old Adriane Yamin, whose mother insisted on acting as chaperone on dates; Senna had no choice but to **acquiesce**

acrostic (noun) = **a poem in which the first letter of each line – when viewed together – forms a word** (*pronounced 'uh-kros-tik'*) from the Greek *akrostikhis*, from *akron*: end + *stikhos*: line of verse

e.g. In the *Dictionary of Modern English Grammar*, Ned Halley defined an acrostic as:

Acrostics are playful
contrivances of prose or verse
rendered so that each line
opens or closes with words in
sequence to read from
top to bottom, their
initial or final letters
constituting a word or phrase.

ad hominem (adj.) = **(of a verbal attack) criticising an opponent's character rather than his policies** (*pronounced 'ad hom-uh-nem'*) from the Latin *ad hominem*: to the person

e.g. Certain political rivals have launched vicious **ad hominem** attacks on Obama, questioning his US citizenship

adamantine (adj.) = **impossible to break** (*pronounced 'ad-uh-man-tie-n'*) from the Greek, *adamas*: untamable, from *a*: not + *daman*: to tame

e.g. Beatrix Potter formed an **adamantine** bond with her nanny's children, and used to write them letters dotted with pictures, which she eventually collected into her first book

adepts (of) (noun) = **a person who is skilled (at something)**
from the Latin *adeptus*: achieved

e.g. Journalists enjoy ridiculing **adepts of** Scientology for their
beliefs

adipose (adj.) = *(of body tissue)* **used for the storage of fat**
(pronounced 'ad-uh-pohs') from the Latin, *adeps, adipis*: fat

e.g. Teenagers who spend all day in front of the TV soon develop
adipose layers around their midriff

to adumbrate (verb) = **to outline** *(pronounced 'ad-uhm-breyt')*
from the Latin *ad-*: to, and *umbrare*: to cast a shadow (from *umbra*:
shade)

e.g. In *Lord of the Flies*, William Golding **adumbrated** the way
society can quickly revert to savagery

agitprop (noun) = **political propaganda,
especially in drama and art** *(pronounced
'aj-it-prop')* from the Russian *agitatsiya*:
agitation, and *propaganda*: propaganda

e.g. Harold Pinter's earlier plays, focusing on
love and power struggles, are much more
popular than the **agitprop** drama of his later
years

akimbo (adv.) = *(of arms)* **with hands on the
hips and elbows turned outward in a
V-formation;** *(of legs)* **flung out wildly** from the
Middle English *in*: in, and *kenebowe*: bend

e.g. If you come across a celebrity in a bar, you will
normally see a bodyguard beside them, dressed
in black and with arms **akimbo**

alarmist (adj.) = **causing needless alarm** from the Old French
alarme: alarm, from Italian *allarme*, from *all'arme!*: to arms!

e.g. Some scientists say talk of global warming is **alarmist**

albatross (around the neck) (set phrase) = **a source of annoyance or guilt** *for full explanation, see box below*

e.g. Pavarotti was known as 'the king of cancellations' and – as he often pulled out of events at the very last minute – often ended up as an **albatross** for organisers

---

This metaphorical sense of 'albatross' derives from Coleridge's poem Rime of the Ancient Mariner *(1798), which features a sailor who shoots an albatross dead.*

After the shooting, the guilty sailor in the poem is then forced to wear the bird's carcass everywhere he goes – as a sign that he alone, and not the rest of the crew, was responsible for the death of the albatross (which was traditionally seen as a good-luck charm).

And so an albatross becomes an encumbrance for the sailor, and entered the language as a metaphor for a source of negative emotion.

---

ambit (noun) = **the scope of something** from the Latin, *ambitus*: circuit, from *ambire*: to go around

e.g. After he turned 40, he decided that any girl between the ages of 20 and 40 fell within his dating **ambit**

amour fou (set phrase) = **an uncontrollable passion**
(pronounced 'amore foo') from the French, *amour fou*: insane love

e.g. *Romeo and Juliet* is Shakespeare's classic tale of **amour fou**: the two lovers cannot give up their liaison, even though they know it will result in their deaths

-ana (suffix) = *(put at the end of another word)* **denoting things associated with a person or with a subject** from the neuter plural of the Latin adjectival ending *-anus*

e.g. Harry Houdini died in 1926, but his props – such as his Chinese Water Torture Cell – are still actively sought out by collectors of Houdini**ana**

anagnorisis (noun) = **the moment in the plot when the hero makes a discovery that explains what he did not understand before** *(pronounced 'an-ag-nawr-uh-sis')* from the Greek *anagnorisis*: recognition; *for full explanation, see box below*

e.g. Boris Johnson has said that Greece has experienced hubris and nemesis but now needs **anagnorisis**: the recognition it would be better off abandoning the euro

---

In Aristotle's Poetics, *there are several stages for a hero to go through; and the classics scholar and Mayor of London Boris Johnson summarised these in an article about the Greek debt crisis entitled* The greatest gift to the Greeks might be to let them go it alone:

'...we have had hamartia – the tragic flaw in the system that allowed high-spending countries to free ride on low interest rates. We have had the hubris – the belief the good times would never end. We have had nemesis – disaster. We now need the anagnorisis – the moment of recognition that Greece would be better off in a state of Byronic liberation, forging a new economic identity with a New Drachma. Then there will be catharsis, the experience of purgation and relief.'

---

analogue (noun) = **a thing comparable to another thing** from the Greek, *analogos*: proportionate

e.g. The English phrase 'self-deprecation' has no **analogue** in the French language: cynics say that, for French people, no such concept exists

to anatomise (verb) = **to dissect in detail** from the Greek *ana-*: up, and *tomia*: cutting

e.g. *Fifty Shades of Grey* **anatomises** the sadomasochistic relationship between a college graduate, Anastasia Steele, and a manipulative billionaire, Christian Grey

anhedonic (adj.) = **unable to feel pleasure** *(pronounced 'an-hee-doh-nik')* from the Greek, *an*: without + *hedone*: pleasure

e.g. In *Winnie the Pooh*, Eeyore is an 'old grey donkey' who wanders around emitting an **anhedonic** listlessness

animadversion (noun) = *(formal)* **a critical statement** from the Latin, *animadvertere*: to criticise, from *animus*: mind + *advertere*, from *a*: toward, and *vertere*: to turn

e.g. Germany's approach to the euro has been subjected to severe **animadversion** by Southern countries desperate for greater financial assistance

antic (adj.) = **grotesque and strange** from the 16th-century Italian *antico*: antique (with the connotation of 'grotesque')

e.g. One of the reasons why sculptor Auguste Rodin is so celebrated is that his statues appear far from static, emitting an **antic** energy

antonym (noun) = **a word that is opposite in meaning to another word** from the French, *antonyme*, from the Greek, *ant-*, from *anti*: against + *onuma*: a name

e.g. Militant atheists see religion as the **antonym** of tolerance

aperçu (noun) = **an illuminating comment** (*pronounced 'a-per-su'*) from the French *apercevoir*: to perceive

e.g. Author Theodor Seuss Geisel aka Dr Seuss had no children of his own; when asked why, he'd deliver this **aperçu**, 'You have 'em; I'll entertain 'em.'

apotropaic (adj.) = **supposedly possessing the power to avert bad luck** (*pronounced 'ap-uh-truh-pey-ik'*) from the Greek, *apotropaios*: averting evil, from *apotrepein*: to turn away from

e.g. After a person dies, the calming funeral service serves an **apotropaic** function

appurtenances (pl. noun) = **an item associated with a particular activity** from the Old French *apertenance*, from the Latin, *appertinere*: to belong to

e.g. Men who work in finance are often obsessed with acquiring yachts and other **appurtenances** of wealth

aquiline (adj.) = *(of a nose)* **curved or hooked, in a similar way to an eagle's beak** from the Latin *aquila*: an eagle

e.g. Abraham Lincoln sported a fine **aquiline** nose

arabesque (noun) = **an ornamental design composed of intertwined flowing lines (originally found in Arabia); or (of ballet) a posture in which the body is supported on one leg, while the other leg is kept flat and extended backward** from the Italian *arabesco*: in the Arabic style, referring to ornamental Moorish architecture and to musical work with an ornamental theme, from *arabo*: Arab

e.g. When it's very cold, **arabesques** of snowflakes alight on your overcoat and dissolve or, the audience gasped as the male ballet dancer lifted his female counterpart in **arabesque**

to arraign (verb) = **to call (someone) before a court to answer a criminal allegation** *(pronounced 'uh-reyn')* from the Latin, *ad*: to, and *ration-*: reason

e.g. After Bruce Lee's son, Brandon, was shot dead on the set of *The Crow*, the fellow actor who'd fired the bullet was not **arraigned** as it was clearly an accident (a live cartridge had been left in the chamber by mistake)

arrant (adj.) = **complete and utter** from the Middle English, a variant of *'errant'* (meaning 'travelling'), originally in phrases such as *'an arrant thief'*, meaning *'a roving thief'*, then, in time, *'a total thief'*

e.g. When the fawning North Korean media reported in 2010 that Kim Jong Il's distinctive jumpsuits had set fashion trends in the West, European journalists dismissed these claims as **arrant** nonsense

to arrogate (a right) (verb) = **to claim (a right) without good cause** *(pronounced 'ar-uh-geyt')* from the Latin *arrogare*: to claim for oneself, from *ad*: to, and *rogare*: to ask

e.g. Alfred Hitchcock **arrogated** the right to appear in every film he directed; in *Strangers on a Train*, for example, you can see him struggling to get a double bass onto a train

asperity (noun) = **(of someone's manner) roughness** from the Latin *asperitas*: roughness, from *asper*: rough

e.g. One way of stopping a compliment from sounding too cloying is to deliver it with some **asperity** in your voice

(set in) aspic (set phrase) = **to be perfectly preserved from an earlier era** *for full etymology, see box below*

e.g. Some men over 70 have an attitude towards women that seems **set in aspic**

The phrase 'set in aspic' literally refers to food – such as leftover chicken – that's been set in a mould of 'aspic', a kind of savoury jelly that dates from the Middle Ages.

In fact, 'aspic' is originally a French word, deriving from 'asp', referring to the asp snake, a viper with similar colouring to the jelly.

Today, when we say of a person or situation that they're 'set in aspic', we mean that they're frozen in the past.

---

astringent (adj.) = *(of someone's manner)* **severe;** *(of a taste)* **sharp** from the Latin *astringere*: to pull tight, from *ad*: toward, and *stringere*: to pull tight

e.g. Whereas certain politicians found Margaret Thatcher's style **astringent**, the late Alan Clark MP found her ways positively arousing (a fact he documented in his diaries)

to attenuate (verb) = **to reduce the effect of** from Latin, *attenuare*: to make slender, from *ad-*: to, and *tenuare*: to make thin; *'to attenuate' literally means 'to make thin'*

e.g. Cynics say the best way to **attenuate** heartache is to kiss someone else

au courant (adj.) = **up-to-date with events** *(pronounced 'au-kur-ohn')* from the French *au courant*: in the (regular) course

e.g. Before directing *Raging Bull*, Martin Scorcese went to numerous boxing matches, so as to be **au courant** with details like 'the blood sponge' to wipe away blood

autarky / autarchy (noun) = **an entity that is economically independent** *(pronounced 'aw-tar-kee')* from the Greek *autarkes*: self-sufficiency, from *autos*: self and *-arkhein*: to suffice

e.g. With its refusal to deal with other countries, North Korea is perhaps the last remaining **autarky** in the world

(an) avatar (of)

(an) avatar (of) (noun) = **an embodiment (of)** from the Sanskrit, *avatar*: descent, from *ava*: down + *tar-*: cross

e.g. For film buffs, John Wayne remains an **avatar** of alpha masculinity

to aver (verb) = **to state to be the case** *(pronounced 'uh-ver')* from the Old French, *averer*: to aver, based on the Latin, *ad*: to (implying 'cause to be') + *verus*: true

e.g. Bruce Lee's name meant 'return again' in Cantonese; his mother chose it as she **averred** her son would one day return to the United States (where he was born), and she was proved right

avowedly (+ adj.) (adv.) = **openly confessing to being (+ adj.)** from the Old French, *avouer*: to acknowledge, from the Latin, *advocare*: to summon in defence

e.g. When his ex-wife started dating billionaire Ted Turner, Pulitzer Prize-winning author Robert Olen Butler wrote in an email, 'She will not be Ted's only girlfriend. Ted is permanently and **avowedly** non-monogamous.'

bagatelle (noun) = **a trifling matter** from the French *bagatelle*: a knick-knack (a small worthless object)

e.g. Compared to his frequent infidelities, she regarded his habit of burping at breakfast time as a mere **bagatelle**

bailiwick (noun) = **a person's area of authority or skill (literally meaning 'the area over which a *bailiff* has power')** *(pronounced 'bay-lee-wik')* from the Old English *bailiff*: bailiff, and *wic*: village

e.g. Critics of Richard Dawkins say that theology is not his **bailiwick**, and he should stick to science

Balkanised (adj.) = *(of a formerly larger entity)* **divided up into smaller parts that are mutually hostile** *(pronounced 'bawl-kuh-nysed')* for full explanation, see box below

e.g. Europe must achieve full financial unity soon, say critics; or else, the continent will divide up into **Balkanised** segments

---

'Balkanisation' is a term invented to describe the division of the Balkan peninsula (formerly ruled by the Ottoman Empire) into several smaller states during the 19th and early 20th centuries.

After World War I, the term was used to refer to the new states that came about following the destruction of the Austro–Hungarian Empire and the Russian Empire.

Since then, 'Balkanisation' has been used to describe many subjects, ranging from the subdivision of the Internet into enclaves (such as Facebook and Google), to the topic of Scottish independence.

---

banshee (noun) = **a female who wails loudly** *for full explanation, see box below*

e.g. When they strike the tennis ball with their racquet, some female players at Wimbledon emit a **banshee** wail

---

'banshee' is from the Irish 'bean sidhe', from 'bean': 'woman' and 'sith': 'fairy'; in Irish mythology, the 'banshee' is a fairy woman who starts to wail if someone is about to die – hence the banshee was regarded as an omen of death.

The banshees wore white and had white hair, which they brushed with a silver comb. (And the fact that banshees used this comb gave rise to the story in Ireland that, if you see a comb on the ground, you shouldn't pick it up – or else the banshees will take you.)

There have been numerous tales of banshees appearing at pivotal moments in history: for example, in 1437, King James I of Scotland was allegedly approached by a banshee who foretold his imminent murder.

---

to barnstorm (verb) = **to travel around the country, making political speeches or taking part in sporting events** *for full explanation, see box below*

e.g. In the run up to the Presidential election, Obama embarked on a multi-week **barnstorming** tour of America

---

The phrase originated from one particular theatrical troupe's performances in upstate New York barns – usually featuring short action pieces – in 1815, which they supposedly 'took by storm'; it was then extended to encompass any spectacular, from political rallies to plane stunts.

---

baroque (adj.) = **very ornate and extravagant in style** *for full explanation, see box below*

e.g. Fashion designer Gianni Versace was shot dead on 15 July 1997, aged 50, on the steps of his **baroque** Miami Beach mansion as he returned from a morning walk (days later, without revealing his motive, his murderer killed himself)

From the French, 'baroque': designating a pearl of elaborate shape; originally, baroque referred exclusively to a 17th- and 18th-century movement in European architecture, art and music that was marked by extreme ornateness: examples include the palace of Versailles, Caravaggio's paintings and Handel's music. In time, the term has come to refer to all elaborate objects and styles, from any century.

basilisk stare (set phrase) = **a stare like a basilisk lizard's (i.e. a look that is keen and malignant)** *(pronounced 'bas-uh-lisk') for full explanation, see box below*

e.g. Bruce Lee's reflexes were so sharp that he could snatch a coin off a person's open palm before they could even close their hand – and leave a penny of his own behind; yet it was not Lee's speed, but his **basilisk stare** that truly petrified opponents

A basilisk is a mythical reptile, believed to have been hatched from a toad's egg placed underneath a cockerel; it had two heads (with the second one – a dragon's head – at the end of its tail) and could kill with a single glance. According to legend, it would expire itself if it looked at itself in the mirror. In Shakespeare's Richard III, *one woman – desiring her enemy's death – says she wishes she had the eyes of a basilisk, that she might kill him. And in* Harry Potter and the Chamber of Secrets, *the basilisk is described as a large dragon, whose direct glare kills instanteously.*

to beard (verb) = **to confront aggressively** from the Middle Dutch, *baert*: a beard, ultimately from the Latin *barba*: beard; *'to beard' literally meant 'to seize by the beard' in medieval times (along the lines of our modern slang, 'to get in someone's face')*

e.g. When he heard that details of Watergate had leaked out, Nixon **bearded** his aides, demanding an explanation

beatitude (noun) = **ultimate blessedness** from the Latin, *beatitudo*: blessedness

e.g. After a big dinner, there is nothing better than lighting a cigar to cement the feeling of self-satisfied **beatitude**

beau monde (noun) = **fashionable society** *(pronounced 'boe monde')* from the 17th-century French, *beau monde*: fine world

e.g. Dentists' waiting rooms teem with magazines carrying paparazzi snaps of the **beau monde** of the famous

becalmed (adj.) = **stuck** from the English words, *be-* + *calm*; *'becalmed' is a nautical term in orgin, with a 'becalmed' ship one that is stuck owing to there being no wind to propel it (and hence one that has been 'made calm')*

e.g. Following the recession of 2008, the normally buoyant New York housing market was **becalmed**

bête noire (noun) = **something or someone that one particularly abhors** *(pronounced 'bet nwar')* from the French, *bête noire*: black beast

e.g. The five-year-old Alfred Hitchcock was once sent by his father to the local police station – with a note asking the officer to lock him up for 10 minues as punishment for behaving badly; thereafter, the young Hitchcock viewed his father as a **bête noire**

biddable (adj.) = **docile and ready to follow another's bidding** from the Old English *beodan*: to command

e.g. On their first date, he plied her with alcohol in the hope drink would make her more **biddable**

bien pensant (adj.) = **holding generally accepted views** *(pronounced 'bee-an pon-son')* from the French *bien*: well, and *pensant*, participle of *penser*: to think; *'bien pensant' literally means 'right-thinking'*

e.g. English actors who make it in Hollywood often turn into **bien pensant** tree-huggers

bildungsroman (noun) = **a novel covering one person's formative years** *(pronounced 'bil-doongz-roh-mahn')* from the German *bildung*: education, and *roman*: a novel

e.g. J.D Salinger's *The Catcher in the Rye* – which charts the gradual maturing of Holden Caulfield – is perhaps the most famous **bildungsroman** of modern times

billet-doux (noun) = *(humorous in tone)* **love letter** (*pronounced 'bill-ay dou'*) from the French, *billet doux*: sweet note

e.g. The *Peanuts* cartoon strip – which made artist Charles M. Schulz over $1bn – was one long **billet-doux** to its canine inspiration: Schulz's family dog, Spike, who loved ingesting metal pins

bleeding heart (noun) = *(derogatory in tone)* **a person so sympathetic – or so politically liberal – that they are considered dangerously softhearted** *'bleeding heart' was originally a direct evocation of Christ – specifically to the bleeding heart under the cross – and His ability to sympathise*

e.g. *Ben-Hur* actor Charlton Heston was famously pro-gun ownership, and considered anyone with an opposing view to be a **bleeding heart** liberal

blowsy (adj.) = *(of a woman)* **messy and red-faced** (*pronounced 'blou-zee'*) from the obsolete expression, *blowze*: a beggar's female companion

e.g. Celebrity gossip magazines take photos of ageing female movie stars, then dissect their **blowsy** faces by circling spots and wrinkles with red ink

bogey (noun) = **a person or thing that evokes fear** (*pronounced 'boh-gee'*) from the Middle English, *bogge*: a frightening ghost; *'bogey' was popularised in World War II as aviator slang to describe an aircraft that wasn't 100 per cent identifiable, but was probably the enemy*

e.g. Sad to say, since her divorce, her ex-husband has become her **bogey**

bosky (adj.) = **covered with bushes** (*pronounced 'bos-kee'*) from the Middle English *bosk*, a variant of *bush*

e.g. In the film *Remains of the Day*, the butler, Stevens – played by Anthony Hopkins – spends much time in the country, driving down **bosky** lanes

brass neck

brass neck (noun) = **gall** *this simile evolved by drawing a comparison between confidence of behaviour and the hardness of brass (just as 'bold as brass' means 'completely unabashed')*

e.g. In 1988 two gunmen wearing ski masks had the **brass neck** to break into the home of *Peanuts* creator Charles M. Schulz, aiming to kidnap his wife Jean; but the attempt was foiled when the couple's daughter, Jill, drove up to the house, scaring off the assailants

Brechtian (adj.) = *(of a play)* **attempting to effect social change and audience participation by continually reminding the audience it is watching a play, and so never allowing the audience to relax** *(pronounced 'brek-tee-on') for full explanation, see box below*

e.g. Most Hollywood film directors aim to create a fictional world for the audience to escape into – rather than to achieve a **Brechtian** alienation effect

---

Bertolt Brecht (1898–1956) was a famous German playwright whose plays are even more popular in Germany than Shakespeare's (in terms of number of annual performances played). His most famous play is The Life of Galileo, *which provided Brecht with a typically strong social theme: the conflict between Galileo (representing scientific evidence) and the Catholic Church (standing for dogmatism).*

Brecht is famous for a theory of theatre called 'the epic theatre' that attempted to instil the need for social change. He differed from other playwrights in that he refused to allow the audience to identify with the actors on the stage, fearing that this would produce complacency (and hence no desire to effect social change). His plan was instead to get the audience to adopt a critical perspective so that they would be more alert to social injustice and so more likely to leave the theatre intent on enacting social improvements.

Various techniques were used by Brecht to remind the spectator that the play is a representation of reality (and not reality itself), such as having actors speak stage directions out loud, and showing the audience explanatory placards.

brickbat (noun) = **an offensive comment** from the English words, *brick + bat; 'brickbat' originally referred to a piece of brick used as a missile, then, in the 17th century, it assumed its current, figurative usage*

e.g. Evangelical Christians who stand on street corners and shout into tannoys, are often exposed to **brickbats** from passers-by

(to secure a) bridgehead (noun) = **(to secure) an area within hostile territory, a base to hold on to, until further troops arrive as backup** *a 'bridgehead' literally refers to a post taken at the end of a bridge nearest to the enemy, both to ensure the bridge's preservation, and to prevent the enemy from crossing*

e.g. In the 1930s, the Nazis expanded into Brazil, believing that the one million German settlers there would make it easy to secure a **bridgehead** against US influence

(to) brocade (something) with (verb) = **to weave (something) with a rich fabric** *(pronounced 'broh-keyd')* from the Italian *broccato*: embossed cloth

e.g. Official biographers of Kim Jong Il **brocaded** the story of his birth **with** such details as a double rainbow spontaneously appearing across the sky at precisely that moment

bromide (noun) = **a trite remark intended to pacify** *(pronounced 'broh-myde') 'bromide' originally referred to a sedative containing potassium bromide; the phrase then went on to assume the figurative meaning of a 'soothing – but trite – expression'*

e.g. After Ayrton Senna's fatal crash, no amount of **bromides** from Brazil's politicians could stem the country's tide of grief: three million people, the largest ever gathering of mourners, flocked to the streets of Senna's hometown, São Paulo

to bruit (verb) = **(of a piece of information) to spread widely** *(pronounced 'broot')* from the Old French, *bruit*: a noise, from *bruire*: to roar

e.g. Heath Ledger was a great chess player, winning Western Australia's junior chess championship at the age of 10: a fact the self-deprecating actor chose not to **bruit**

buccaneer

buccaneer (noun) = **bold, adventurous and, at times, reckless**
(pronounced 'buk-uh-neer') for full explanation, see box below

e.g. Even though he turned Apple into the biggest technology company in the world, Steve Jobs somehow managed to retain the air of a Silicon Valley **buccaneer**

'buccaneer' derives from the French 'boucanier': a user of a 'boucan' (a West Indian grill for roasting meat), specifically referring to those French hunters who, in the 1690s, stole pigs and cows from the modern-day Haiti and the Dominican Republic, roasting these animals on their grills. When the Spaniards, based in these parts, tried to drive out these troublesome French 'boucaniers', the latter turned to piracy, targeting Spanish ships.

With time, English settlers occupying Jamaica started using the word 'buccaneer' (adapting the French 'boucanier') to refer to these bold pirates.

(Incidentally, England – in defiance of her enemy, Spain – actually supported these buccaneers and their plundering, since this was an informal way of inflicting damage on Spain, England's enemy: the English crown even went so far as to license the buccaneers with 'letters of marque', actually legitimising their operations in return for a share of the spoils plundered by the pirates from the Spanish ships.)

---

buckshee (adj.) = *(informal in tone)* **free of any charge**
(pronounced 'buk-shee') for full explanation, see box below

e.g. Since the train was running one hour late, the ticket inspector arranged for everyone onboard to receive a **buckshee** Coke

---

'buckshee' was originally World War I soldiers' slang, meaning 'a small amount of money given as a tip or bribe'; 'buckshee' was a variant of the English word 'baksheesh' (which has an identical meaning, and which ultimately derived from the Persian 'baksis', from 'baksidan': to give).

to burnish (verb) = **to perfect** from the Old French *burnir,* a version of *brunir*: to make brown or bright by polishing, from *brun*: brown

e.g. When it was revealed that J. Edgar Hoover, the FBI director, had personally requested an audit of *The Grapes of Wrath* author John Steinbeck's taxes (just to annoy the writer), Hoover's reputation as a difficult man was further **burnished**

C

cack-handed (adj.) = **clumsy** *for full explanation, see box below*

e.g. If you put an average person up against a politician in a debate, the layman will inevitably come across as **cack-handed**

From the Old English, 'cack': 'excrement', from the Latin 'cacare': 'to defecate'; in the not so distant past – and certainly before Andrex and its puppies came along – our ancestors used to use their left hand for cleaning themselves after defecating, whilst (to keep things simple) the right hand was used exclusively for eating with.

To use one's 'cack hand' was therefore to use one's left hand and, since most people are right-handed and struggle to fully control their left hand, being 'cack-handed' meant being 'clumsy'.

---

to be a cakewalk (noun) = **to be a walk in the park** *for full explanation, see box below*

e.g. With a mass influx of people (who were fleeing from communist China), the streets of Hong Kong in the 1950s saw many fights between gangs. Bruce Lee was often on the losing side in these – until he took up martial arts, and then such conflicts became a **cakewalk** for him

From the words 'cake' + 'walk', referring to a dancing competition arranged by slave-owners in the Southern United States in c. 1890–1910. Specifically, the 'cake' was the prize for the most stylish display by a slave couple in this competition; and the 'walk' was the name for the dancing competition itself (which was described as 'a walking competition among negroes' by one writer of the time, Richard Thornton).

This 'cakewalk' was an exaggerated parody of the formal ballroom dancing preferred by the white slave-owners, and was generally considered (by the slave-owners, at any rate) as a fun, recreational pastime.

And so it was that the term 'cakewalk' began to be used, from 1909, to indicate something that is fun, and easy to do. (A 'piece of cake', to denote an effortless activity, shares the same origin.)

to calcify (into something) (verb) = **to turn (into something) more solid** *(pronounced 'kal-suh-fy')* from the French *calcifier*: to calcify, from the Latin *calcem*: lime (the oxide of the metallic base calcium)

e.g. When faith **calcifies into** closed-mindedness, religious zealotry can result

canard (noun) = **a false rumour** *(pronounced 'ka-nar') for full explanation, see box below*

e.g. After hearing that the *New York Journal* had published an article about his demise, Mark Twain said of this **canard**, 'The reports of my death are greatly exaggerated'

'canard' is the French for 'duck' – and the reason 'canard' means 'false rumour' in English, is because of a strange habit attributed to ducks.

For it's said that, if a predator approaches its young, a parent duck will draw the foe away by feigning a broken wing, depicting themselves as the easier target. When the predator gets near the apparently injured duck, the bird takes off (and, meanwhile – with the enemy thus distracted – the young ducks have also hopefully taken flight).

In other words, the duck is lying (to the predator); and a 'canard' means a big fat lie of a rumour.

to stand like Canute against the tide

to stand like Canute against the tide (verb) = **to believe you have the power to prevent an impending catastrophe when you are in fact powerless** (pronounced 'ka-<u>noot</u>') for full explanation, see box below

e.g. If a woman is hellbent on getting a divorce, then she will get her way; and any husband who tries to stop her is **standing like Canute against the tide**

Canute the Great (985–1035), King of England, Denmark, Norway and Sweden, was famous for having his courtiers bring his throne to a beach and then – apparently to show his omnipotence – commanding the tide to halt in its tracks (before it could wet his feet and robes). Naturally the waves completely ignored his order and splashed all over the king, drenching him.

Twelfth-century historian Henry of Huntingdon tells us what happened next: 'Then the king leapt backwards, saying: "Let all men know how empty and worthless is the power of kings, for there is none worthy of the name, but He whom heaven, earth, and sea obey by eternal laws." He then hung his gold crown on a crucifix, and never wore it again "to the honour of God the almighty King". For Canute was no fool and had in fact performed this stunt to show his obsequious courtiers that – despite their claims to the contrary – he did not possess the gift of omnipotence.'

However, popular culture continues to misrepresent this incident, depicting Canute as being arrogant and genuinely believing all along that the ocean would obey him. So, if you say of someone today that they are 'standing like Canute against the tide', you are saying they are self-delusional and wrongly believe they possess the necessary skills to stop an imminent disaster – when the events they are trying to stop, are in fact totally out of their control.

---

capstone (noun) = **a crowning achievement** from the English words *cap* + *stone*, referring literally to the topmost stone in a construction

e.g. Patricia Highsmith's novel *The Talented Mr Ripley* was the **capstone** of her career

to carouse (verb) = **to drink to excess but joyfully** *(pronounced 'kuh-rouz')* from the Old German *gar aus trinken*: to drink heavily, from *gar aus*: all out, *trinken*: to drink; *the original English expression was 'to drink carouse', then 'to carouse'*

e.g. James Joyce's relentless **carousing** was punctuated by bouts of writing

carrion (noun) = **the rotting flesh of dead animals** *(pronounced 'kar-ee-uhn')* from the Old French, *charoigne*, based on the Latin, *caro*: flesh

e.g. My uncle buried his dead Alsatian in the garden, and a few days later, the **carrion** had attracted a family of worms

caryatid (noun) = *(in architecture)* **a supporting pillar that has been carved into a female shape** *(pronounced 'kar-ee-at-id')* for full explanation, see box below

e.g. Caryatids placed on either side of a fireplace look a bit naff

---

The term 'caryatid' derives from the Greek 'Karyatides', meaning 'maidens of Caryae (a town in Greece)'. In this town 'Caryae', there was a famous temple dedicated to the goddess Artemis, where maidens performed elaborate dances in Artemis's honour.

During the dances, the maidens of 'Caryae' would move around violently whilst all the while carrying atop their heads baskets of live reeds.

Hence the architectural term 'caryatid' evolved, to describe pillars carved into the shape of a woman's body, with the woman's head – which is, of course, at the top of the pillar – therefore seeming to hold up the roof (which rests on the pillar/head). This is an echo of the female dancers in Caryae using their heads to support baskets.

---

caste (noun) = **a distinct social class (determined from birth);** *(pronounced 'cast')* from the Spanish, *casta*: lineage

e.g. Critics say that, in the United States, it is only those individuals who have received an expensive education that end up in highly paid jobs in banks and law firms, allowing them in turn to pay for their own children's expensive education and perpetuate the cycle: evidence that an unofficial **caste** system still operates **27**

casuistic (noun) = **clever but intellectually dishonest – often by being overly pedantic** *(pronounced '<u>kas</u>-oo-is-tik') for full explanation, see box below*

e.g. Barristers who defend patently guilty serial killers in court, must be ashamed of the **casuistic** distinctions they have recourse to, when they defend their despicable clients

---

'casuistic' is from the French 'casuiste': 'one who studies case of conscience', and ultimately from the Latin 'casus': 'a case of conscience'. The term 'casuistic' started life meaning 'pursuing case-based reasoning' – usually in the realms of law and ethics – as opposed to 'rule-based reasoning'. Western casuistry dates from Aristotle (384–322 BC) and – in its original form – worked by extracting theoretical rules from a particular instance (or 'case') and then applying them to new instances, so as to resolve moral dilemmas.

'Casuistic' reasoning reached its peak of popularity between 1550 and 1650, when (Roman Catholic) Jesuit priests championed case-based reasoning, particularly when administering the Sacrament of Penance (also known as 'confession'). However, philosopher Blaise Pascal (1623–62) pointed out that the Jesuits were misusing 'casuistic' reasoning to justify giving lighter punishments in confession to the rich (whose financial contributions were so important to the Church), whilst doling out heavier penalties to the poor (who had no money to donate). These criticisms of Pascal turned 'casuistic' into a dirty word.

Today, this pejorative sense persists, with 'casuistic' being used to refer to someone who twists the facts – in a clever but intellectually false way – to make a point.

---

cataract (noun) = **a downpour;** *the other meaning in English is, of course, 'a lens of the eye that has become opaque, resulting in blurred vision' (the link to 'downpour' here is that rapidly running water turns white, and the medical condition turns the eye white)* from the Greek *kataraktes*: down-striking, from *kara-*: down, and *arassein*: strike

e.g. On their first dinner date, she peered out at him from behind **cataracts** of curls

catarrh (noun) = **a build-up of mucus in the nose and throat** *(pronounced 'kuh-tar')* from the Greek *katarrhous*: a head cold, from *kata-*: down, and *rhein*: to flow

e.g. No one will want to kiss you when you've got a **catarrh**-filled mouth from the flu

catechism (noun) = **a set of rules (or of questions and answers), used for instruction** *(pronounced 'kat-i-kiz-uhm')* from the Greek, *katekhein*: to instruct by word of mouth

e.g. Critics say socialism's **catechism** amounts to little more than an ever-expanding welfare state

(to be) catnip (to someone) (verb) = *(of an object)* **to drive someone wild** *'catnip' is the informal name for 'nepeta', a flowering plant known for driving cats crazy (owing to a substance in the plant binding to the olfactory receptors of the cat)*

e.g. Mobile phones are **catnip** to toddlers, who love a well-lit screen

to caucus (verb) = **to hold a meeting of a group of people with shared concerns** *(pronounced 'kor-kis')* from the Native American *caucauasu*: gathering of tribal chiefs

e.g. The coffee during the meeting sent us all off to the bathroom, and we ended up **caucusing** much more effectively around the urinals than we had done at the table earlier

chagrin (noun) = **embarrassment at having been publicly humiliated** *(pronounced 'sha-grin')* from the French, *chagrin*: rough skin

e.g. After a few harsh comments from the judges, most *X Factor* rejects slink off stage, their faces a picture of **chagrin**

changeling (noun) = **a baby who looks so unlike its parents that it must be an imposter (substituted for the parents' actual baby, by mischevious fairies)** from the English word *change*, combined with the diminutive suffix -*ling*

e.g. The blonde couple were surprised when their child was born with jet-black hair; and they joked to their friends that their baby was a **changeling**

chary (of) (adj.) = **cautious (about)** (*pronounced 'chair-ee'*) *from the Old English, 'cearig': 'sorrowful', related to 'care'; 'chary' started to be used in the mid-16th century*

e.g. Children are advised to be **chary of** strangers

chiaroscuro (noun) = **the interplay of light and shade on a surface** (*pronounced 'kee-ar-uh-roskuro'*) *from the Italian, chiaro: clear (from the Latin clarus) and oscuro: dark (from the Latin obscurus)*

e.g. When sunlight hits a running stream, a pleasing **chiaroscuro** results

chiliastic / millenarian (adj.) = **believing in the imminence of a golden age (originally one lasting 1,000 years)** (*'chiliastic' is pronounced 'chil-ay-astic'*) *from the Greek, khilias: a thousand years, from khilioi: thousand; and from the Latin, millenarius: containing a thousand, based on the Latin, mille: thousand; for full explanation, see box below*

e.g. Obama's election to power was greeted with **chiliastic / millenarian** fervour by Democrats

---

'chiliastic' (which derives from the Greek word for 'one thousand') is another word for 'millenarian' (which comes from the Latin word for 'one thousand'). Both words started off referring to a specific religious belief, of a future, thousand-year-long age of blessedness.

For example, Jehovah's Witnesses allegedly believe that the current world era entered the 'last days' in October 1914, and that soon Armageddon (the final battle between Christ and the Devil) will come. And, once Armageddon is out of the way, Christ will rule over the earth – which will be transformed into a paradise similar to the Garden of Eden – for 1,000 years.

But over time, the phrase 'chiliastic' or 'millenarian' evolved to refer to a much more general (not necessarily religious) belief in a golden age of peace and prosperity (of no specified timeframe).

---

chthonic (adj.) = **from hell; from the underworld (literally: dwelling beneath the surface of the earth) (note: the pronunciation is simply 'thonic': the 'ch-' is silent)** from the Greek, khthonios: in the earth (i.e. under the world's surface)

e.g. After he said he wanted a divorce, it was as if a **chthonic** river of repressed rage was suddenly unblocked in her, and she chopped off the right sleeves from all his shirts

chugger (noun) = **a charity mugger (one of those people with a clipboard in the street, who blocks your path and asks if you 'have a minute')** *'chugger' is a conflation of 'charity' and 'mugger' (just like 'Brangelina' is a conflation of 'Brad' and 'Angelina')*

e.g. You cannot move down most high streets in London without being accosted by a beaming **chugger**

cicerone (noun) = **a guide who shows strangers the interesting bits of a place** *(pronounced 'sis-uh-roh-nee') for full explanation, see box below*

e.g. When my Australian cousins visited London, I was happy to act as **cicerone**, showing them my favourite haunts

---

'cicerone' derives from the Latin 'Ciceronem', from the name of ancient Rome's greatest orator, Cicero (106–43 BC).

In fact, Marcus Tulius Cicero delivered speeches of such verve that he became one of the most popular men in ancient Rome, with an unrivalled ablility to whip up the populace into a frenzy. In addition, he was renowned in his lifetime for his distinguished political career and for his philosophical writings, especially on the subject of liberty. But it was not just his own era that Cicero influenced: the French Revolution was started by young people allegedly so enthused by their reading of Cicero that they were moved to violence, to reclaim the liberty spoken of so eloquently by the Roman orator. And Thomas Jefferson (1743–1826) named Cicero as one of several major figures who had created a tradition 'of public right' that informed his draft of the Declaration of Independence (1776).

Cicero was not some academic in an ivory tower: he could be ruthless too, once murdering without trial five men who had threatened to assassinate him (and then overthrow the Roman Republic). So it was no surprise when his own death proved a violent one: his enemy Mark Antony – with whom Cicero was involved in a power struggle following Julius Caesar's death; and against whom Cicero had whipped the people into yet another frenzy with his oratory – had Cicero decapitated. Then Antony's wife ripped Cicero's tongue from his severed head and jabbed it over and over with her hairpin, in final revenge against Cicero's renowned eloquence. But his name lives on today, as a tribute to anyone with great powers of speech ('Ciceronian'), or to credit a guide with great wisdom (as a 'cicerone').

Ciceronian (adj.) = **eloquent** *(pronounced 'sis-uh-roh-nee-uhn')* *deriving from the name of the legendary Roman orator Cicero; for full explanation, see box on page 31*

e.g. Enoch Powell said, "You should do nothing to decrease the tension before making a big speech. If anything, you should seek to increase it." This was why Powell – to hit **Ciceronian** heights – delivered speeches on a full bladder

to coarsen (verb) = **to become vulgar and crude; *'to coarsen'*** *literally means 'to make rough, coarse'* from the English word *coarse*, itself deriving from *course*, in the sense of 'ordinary in manner'

e.g. Some parents blame the expletive-ridden lyrics of rappers for **coarsening** their children's language

cod- (prefix) = **fake** *'cod-' is an abbreviation of 'cod-head', an expression used to describe someone who had so little sense that it was as though they had the head of a codfish; this connotation of mindless emptiness then went on to mean 'without substance', or, 'fake'*

e.g. Critics of John Fowles' novel *The Magus* – the story of a young English teacher who discusses the paradoxical nature of life with a much older Greek intellectual – accuse Fowles of filling his pages with **cod-**philosophising

codicil (noun) = **a supplementary clause** *(pronounced 'code-uh-sil')* from the Latin, *codicillus*: a short piece of writing, the diminutive of *codex*: a book

e.g. Many people seek fame; but they may not be familiar with fame's **codicil** – which is that, once you're famous, you're constantly harassed by people

to codify (a situation) (verb) = **to arrange (a situation) into a set of codes and rules** from the English words, *code* + *-fy*: a suffix meaning *to make into*, from the French, *-fier*, ultimately from the Latin, *-ficare*, itself from the verb *facere*: to make

e.g. Increasingly, governments are setting up committees to **codify** an official stance towards euthanasia

cognitive dissonance (noun) = **the state of having inconsistent beliefs, usually about one's own behaviour** *for full explanation, see box below*

e.g. An evangelical Christian who loses both arms in a car accident, may well experience some **cognitive dissonance** as he tries to reconcile a loving deity with his new disfigurement

---

'cognitive dissonance' is a term from psychology, referring to the discomfort felt when you hold two conflicting cognitions (i.e. beliefs) at the same time.

Psychologists have the view that people who are in this state (i.e. most of us), are then likely to reduce dissonance by altering their existing beliefs – by, for example, lying to themselves that one of the ideas that is in conflict with the other is not very important (even when they know that it is, in fact, very important).

The classic example is that of the smoker, who wants to smoke, yet knows that smoking is unhealthy; in this situation, the smoker is then likely to lie to himself, by saying it is very unlikely that the ill effects of smoking will befall him in particular. (Hence, one definition of cognitive dissonance is when one is biased towards a certain decision – in this case, to keep on smoking – even though other factors favour the alternative course, namely to give up smoking since smoking can do you harm.)

---

collation (noun) = **a light, relaxed meal** from the Latin, *collation-*, from *conferre*, from *con-*: together, and *ferre*: to bring

e.g. When my uncle turned up unexpectedly, I managed to transform the roast chicken left over from lunch into a nice **collation** for us both

to collectivise (something) (verb) = **to organise (something) on the basis of ownership by the state, abolishing private ownership** from the English words, *collective + -ise*

e.g. Critics say a socialist government will **collectivise** the nation's resources and thus undermine the capitalist impulse

colloquium (noun) = **a meeting for the discussion of a subject** (*pronounced 'kuh-low-kwee-uhm'*) from the Latin *colloqui*: to converse, from *col-*: together, and *loqui*: to talk

e.g. Saddam Hussein tended to kill rivals on a whim – rather than holding a **colloquium** to discuss the subject

comity (noun) = **social harmony** (*pronounced 'kom-i-tee'*) from the Latin *comis*: courteous

e.g. Even if a marriage is bursting with mutual animosity, often in public the couple will emit some semblance of **comity**

commentariat (noun) = **members of the news media, viewed as a collective** (*pronounced 'com-en-tair-i-at'*) from a blend of the English words *commentary* + *proletariat*

e.g. After it became clear the UK public seemed to be revelling in the Pope's visit, the **commentariat** did a volte-face, dishing out praise – instead of their initial vitriol – towards the pontiff

compendious (adj.) = **(of a book) succinctly containing all the essential facts** (pronounced *'kuhm-pen-dee-uhs'*) from the Latin, *compendiosus*: advantageous, from *compendium*: abbreviation

e.g. Ernst Gombrich's bestseller *A Little History of the World* – originally intended for children but often read secretly by adults – is a **compendious** account of the past

to concertina (into) (verb) = **to compress (into) (like you do with a 'concertina', a musical instrument that is hand-held, with a bellows in the middle)** (*pronounced 'kon-ser-tee-nuh'*) the term *'concertina' was apparently coined by the original instrument's inventor, Englishman Charles Wheatstone (1802–75)*

e.g. The novel *Never Let Me Go* is about a group of human clones created to provide organs for non-clones, and who therefore die young (when their last organ has been harvested); much poignancy results from their lives being **concertinaed into** this shorter-than-usual lifespan

concupiscent (adj.) = **lustful** (*pronounced 'kon-kyoo-pi-suhnt'*) from the Latin, *concupiscent-*: looking for, coveting, from the Latin, *concupiscere*: to look for, covet

e.g. Whilst President of the United States, JFK was as **concupiscent** as a rabbit

condign (adj.) = *(of a punishment)* **deserved** *(pronounced 'kuhn-dahyn')* from the Latin *con-* (which expresses intensive force), and *dignus*: worthy

e.g. In America, most states continue to execute murderers, as this is considered **condign** punishment for the taking of a life

to condole with (someone) (verb) = **to express sympathy for (someone)** from the Latin, *condolere*, from *con-*: with + *dolere*: to suffer

e.g. After Roger Federer beat Andy Murry to win a record seventh Wimbledon title, Federer's reaction was to **condole with** his foe, putting an arm around him

confederacy (noun) = **a group of people united by a league** from the Latin, *confoedarare*: to join together in league, from *con-*: together + *foederare*: to join in league with, from *foedus*: league

e.g. Jonathan Swift (1667–1745), author of *Gulliver's Travels*, once said, 'When a true genius appears in the world, you may know him by this sign, that the dunces are all in **confederacy** against him'

conflagration (noun) = **a destructive fire** *(pronounced 'kon-fluh-grey-shuhn')* from the Latin, *con-* (expressing intensive force), and *flagrare*: to blaze

e.g. When the two planes hit the World Trade Centre, a terrible **conflagration** resulted

conjugal / connubial (adj.) = **relating to marriage** *(pronounced 'kon-juh-guhl' / 'kuh-noo-bee-uhl')* 'conjugal' is from the Latin, 'conjug-': 'a spouse', from 'con-': together, 'jugum': 'a yoke'; 'connubial' is from the Latin, 'connubium': 'marriage', from 'con-': with + 'nubere': 'to marry'

e.g. If a woman catches sight of a wedding ring on a man, she's often put off pursuing him – for she has no wish to tempt him from his **conjugal / connubial** duties

constellation (noun) = **a cluster of things related to each other** from the Latin, *constellatio*, based on Latin, *stella*: star; *a 'constellation' literally refers to a group of stars forming a recognisable pattern that is traditionally named after a mythological character or animal*

e.g. The film *Tinker, Tailor, Soldier, Spy* starred a **constellation** of British actors, including Gary Oldman, Colin Firth and Benedict Cumberbatch

consumptive (noun) = **a person with a wasting disease** from the Latin *consumpt-*, from the verb *consumere*: to consume

e.g. In Hollywood films, prostitutes are usually depicted as heroin-addled **consumptives**

contiguous (to) (adj.) = **sharing a boundary (with)** *(pronounced 'kuhn-tig-yoo-uhs')* from the Latin *contiguus*: touching, from *contingere*: to be in contact

e.g. The United States of Amereica is comprised of 48 **contiguous** states

continent (adj.) = **exercising self-control, especially in sexual matters** from the Latin, *continere*: to hold together, restrain oneself, from *con-*: altogether + *tenere*: to hold

e.g. The priest had always prided himself on his **continent** lifestyle

to be co-opted (by) (verb) = **to be adopted (for the use of)** from the Latin, *cooptare*: to choose as a colleague of one's own tribe, from *com-*: together, and *optare*: to choose

e.g. In New York, bingo bars are now full of hipsters: bizarrely, it seems bingo is being **co-opted by** a younger generation

copse (noun) = **a small group of bushes** *(pronounced 'kops')* *copse* is an abbreviation of the English word, *coppice*: a small thicket of trees grown for cutting, deriving from the Old French, *copeiz*: a cut-over forest

e.g. On the backs of some men, **copses** of hair sprout

the Corinthian spirit (set phrase) = *(of a sportsman)* **the very highest standards of sportsmanship** *for full explanation, see box below*

e.g. Roger Federer, with his good manners on and off the court, embodies for many the **Corinthian** spirit

---

The ancient city of Corinth (700–200 BC) was renowned for its huge wealth, which derived from its location: Corinth stood on the narrow stretch of land that joins mainland Greece to the peninsula of the Peloponnese, and so controlled all land access to the Peloponnese, making Corinth a very busy trading city.

And how did the citizens of Corinth – the 'Corinthians' – spend this wealth? On debauched activities, is how. For example, the Temple of Aphrodite was well stocked with more than a thousand 'temple prostitutes', who offered sexual intercourse in the context of religious worship (as a kind of fertility rite). It's no accident that St Paul wrote his letters to the Corinthians – it was they who were most in need of spiritual guidance. In Shakespeare's day, the term 'Corinthian' therefore meant 'licentious'; in fact, Prince Henry (Hal) refers to himself as: 'a Corinthian, a lad of mettle, a good boy' in the play Henry IV, Part I *(c. 1597).*

But in the British Regency era (1812–20), a slight tweak in meaning was applied to the term 'Corinthian', which began to refer to a group of wealthy, hard-living, 'licentious' aristocrats who were also dedicated to sports (particularly horse-racing and yacht-sailing). And by 1900, it was this latter nuance that had taken a full grip on the word 'Corinthian', which by now had lost its hard-living connotations and retained only the idea of gentlemanliness and amateurism; today, the term 'Corinthian spirit' is still used to evoke this idea of maintaining the highest standards in sport (as these amateurs did), and of pursuing sport for the love of the game, rather than for money.

---

counterposed to (set phrase) = *(of an idea)* **set in opposition to** from the English words, *counter* + *pose*

e.g. In the TV adaptation of *Birdsong*, the love story **was counterposed to** violent scenes from World War I

countervailing (something) (adj.) = **offsetting the effect (of something) by countering it with something of equal power** from the Anglo–Norman French, *contrevaloir*, from Latin, *contra valere*: be of worth against; *note that 'countervailing' is very much the cousin of 'prevailing', which comes from the Latin, 'prae': before + 'valere': 'have power', implying a dominance – whereas 'countervailing' implies a stalemate, as the forces in opposition are equal*

e.g. In their live debate, the two Presidential candidates were very evenly matched, and their **countervailing** views meant there was no obvious winner

coup de théâtre (set phrase) = **a dramatically sudden outcome, especially in a play** (*pronounced 'koo-duh-tey-atr-a'*) from the French, *coup de théâtre*: blow of theatre

e.g. The film *The Usual Suspects* finishes with a startling **coup de théâtre**, when the shock identity of the villain is unveiled

(to stick in the) craw (of) (noun) = *(of an unpalatable fact)* **to stick in the throat of** related to the Middle Low German, *krage*: throat

e.g. After she divorced him, what really **stuck in her craw** was that his new wife had bigger breasts than her

creditable (adj.) = *(of an effort)* **deserving credit (but not necessarily outstanding)** *(note this is quite different from 'credible', which means 'able to be believed')* (*pronounced 'kred-i-tuh-buhl'*) from the English words *credit + able*

e.g. That the team's performances have been **creditable** over the last decade is little consolation for Engand football fans, who crave more victories

crinoline (noun) = **a hooped petticoat worn to make a long skirt stand outwards** (*pronounced 'krin-il-in'*) from the French, *crinoline*, from the Latin, *crinis*: hair + *linum*: thread *(since the first crinolines were made from hair and thread)*

e.g. To look the part for TV period dramas, actresses are usually forced to climb into **crinoline**

cupidity (noun) = **greed for money or goods** from the Latin, *cupiditas*: desirousness, from *cupidus*: desirous

e.g. Her New Year's resolution was to stop buying designer labels, but when she stepped into the Gucci superstore, her **cupidity** was once again aroused

curate's egg (set phrase) = *(of a situation)* **something that is in part good, and in part bad** *for full explanation, see box below*

e.g. Certain journalists have called Putin's latest victory a **curate's egg**: for, even if the West might disagree with Putin's interpretation of democracy, Russia will at least be stable under his reign

---

The term derives from a cartoon, drawn by George du Maurier (grandfather of Daphne du Maurier) and published in Punch *magazine on 9 November 1895. Entitled 'True Humility', it pictured a mild-mannered curate, Mr Jones, taking breakfast in the house of his superior, the bishop.*

The bishop remarks with disarming honesty to his guest, 'I'm afraid you've got a bad egg, Mr Jones.' And the curate, the epitome of a man intent on keeping his superior happy, replies, 'Oh, no, my Lord, I assure you that parts of it are excellent!'

In the very final issue of Punch *published in 1992, the cartoon was re-printed with the caption, 'Curate: This f***ing egg's off!' (This was apparently so as to draw a contrast between the Victorian good manners prevalent at the time of the original cartoon, and today's yobbishness.)*

---

curlicue (noun) = **a fancy curl** *from the mid-19th century, a conflation of the words 'curly' (like a 'pigtail') + 'cue' (representing the letter 'q')*

e.g. At weddings, the dinner tables often have placards for guests rendered in black **curlicues** against white card

cursory (adj.) = **hasty, and therefore not thought through** *(note that the way 'cursory' differs from 'perfunctory' is that 'cursory' is speedy, whereas 'perfunctory' need not be; both refer to actions thoughtlessly performed)* from the Latin, *cursorius*: of a runner, from *cursor*: runner

e.g. Jack the Ripper – who usually stole the uterus from his victims before making his escape – was never caught, so he must have given more than a **cursory** glance to the crime scene before he made off, to ensure he left no traces

cyclorama

cyclorama (noun) = **a background to a stage, often depicting a sky** (*pronounced 'sahy-kluh-rahm-uh'*) from *cyclo-*, along the pattern of words like *panorama*

e.g. *The David Letterman Show* **cyclorama** has a metropolitan backdrop, composed of bright lights and tall buildings

cynosure (noun) = **a person or thing that is the centre of attention** (*pronounced '<u>sahyn</u>-uh-shoor'*) *for full explanation, see box below*

e.g. Mother Theresa of Calcutta was for decades the **cynosure** of the poor in India

---

'cynosure' is from the Greek 'kynosoura', meaning 'dog's tail': the name given by the Greeks to one of the brightest stars in the sky (which we now call 'Polaris'). The reason? Well, this star was – and still is – part of a bigger constellation of stars that the Greeks saw as a 'dog', with this particular (very bright) star corresponding to the location of the 'dog's tail'. (Today, this same constellation is known as 'Ursa Minor', meaning 'Smaller Bear' in Latin; as astrologers have now decided that the constellation does, after all, look more like a bear than a dog.)

Because it lies in an almost direct line with the axis of the earth's rotation, the star called 'kynosoura' / 'Polaris' appears to stand almost motionless in the sky, with other stars seeming to rotate around it. In the days before GPS was used (i.e. before 1960), sailors used this star as a guide, because its apparently fixed position meant you could use it to work out where you were on a dark night at sea.

So – because of its importance in this activity of 'celestial navigation' (the posh term for a sailor trying to work out where the hell he is) – the eyes of sailors and travellers were often directed to 'kynosoura', the fixed star. And this is why the word 'cynosure' today means 'a person or object that is the centre of attention'.

40

to have the sword of Damocles hanging over (someone's) head (set phrase) = to have an imminent harm threatening (someone) *('Damocles' is pronounced 'dam-uh-kleez')* *for full explanation, see box below*

e.g. Anyone in charge of a political coalition knows that internal forces might explode it at any moment: such a leader **has the sword of Damocles hanging over him**

Damocles was an obsequious courtier who was always telling Dionysius II, King of Syracuse (397–343 BC), how lucky and happy the king was. To prove to Damocles that this was untrue – that he was not always happy – King Dionysius offered to swap places with Damocles, to show him what being a king was really like.

When Damocles was installed on the throne and enjoying fine wine and food, Dionysius attached to the patch of ceiling above Damocles's head, a sword – held in place by one solitary hair alone, that could snap at any time.

This was to show Damocles the unhappy-making and ever-present peril faced by those in a position of power (from those trying to usurp the ruler); and 'the sword of Damocles' has now come to mean, more generally, the sense of foreboding engendered by a precarious situtation.

---

dance of death / danse macabre (set phrase) = a medieval painting of a dance, with Death (as a skeleton) at the front, leading to their graves a chain of people *(linked together in order of social rank, from an emperor at the front, to a pauper at the end – showing the universality of death)* *('danse macabre' is pronounced 'dahns ma-ka-br-a')* from the French, *danse macabre*: dance of death

e.g. One afternoon, shortly after his aunt and wife had died within days of each other, he found himself staring out of the window, thinking he'd finally seen the world for what it really was: **a dance of death**

darkling (adj.) = *(of a sky)* **growing dark** *from the Middle English, 'dark' + '-ling' (a suffix denoting condition); the verb 'to darkle' – derived from the adjective 'dark' – dates from the 15th century*

e.g. When they notice the **darkling** sky, car drivers turn their lights on

debased (adj.) = *(of a person or situation)* **lowered morally** *(pronounced 'dee-baysd')* from the English words, *de-*: down, and the outdated verb *to base*, which together express the notion: *'to bring down completely'*

e.g. The only retailer consistently left alone by the London rioters was Waterstones; for the yobs had no interest in books: a sure sign of a **debased** culture

déclassé (adj.) = **belonging to a lower social class** *(pronounced 'dey-kla-sey')* from the French, *déclassé*: having lost class, from *de-*: from + *classer*: to class

e.g. Drinking rosé wine – which used to be regarded as **déclassé** – has suddenly become socially acceptable

decorous (adj.) = **seemly**; *literally meaning, 'exhibiting decorum'* *(pronounced 'dek-er-uhs')* from the Latin, *decorus*: seemly

e.g. In Scottish reeling, a **decorous** space between dancing partners is observed at all times

defenestrated (noun) = *(of an authority figure)* **suddenly removed from power;** *literally meaning 'the act of throwing someone out of the window'* *(pronounced 'dee-fen-uh-strey-ted')* *– hence 'defenestrated', being such an over-the-top image, is always comical in tone for full explanation, see box below*

e.g. Opponents of the monarchy would like to see the Queen removed; a few extremists would doubtless like to see her **defenestrated**

'defenestrated' derives from the Latin, 'de-': 'out of' + 'fenestra': 'window'.

Historically, the concept of 'defenestration' was used to refer to an act of political dissent – specifically, 'the Defenestration of Prague' in 1618, a time when the rights of Protestants were being curtailed by Catholics. The individuals subject to the actual chucking from the window (or 'defenestration') in question were three prominent Catholics, who were suspected by the Protestants of writing a letter to the king ordering that no more Protestant churches be built on royal land. In the event, these three Catholics survived being pushed out of the third-floor window – and the ensuing fall of some 20 metres – owing to their thick coats, and to the uneven castle walls (that blunted their descent).

The most poignant case of defenestration in modern times is perhaps that of Garry Hoy (1955–93), a lawyer best known for the circumstances of his death. In an attempt to prove to a group of his partners at his law firm that the glass in the building was unbreakable, Hoy threw himself against a glass wall on the 24th storey, only for the window frame to yield. For his unusual death, Hoy was recognised with a Darwin Award in 1996.

to defray (a cost) (verb) = **to pay (a cost)** (*pronounced 'dih-frey'*) from the French, *défrayer*, from *dé-*: expressing removal + (*now obsolete*) *frai*: cost

e.g. The businessman gave the prostitute – who had visited him in his hotel – a fifty pound note to **defray** her taxi fare home

to delineate (something) (verb) = **to outline (something) in words or drawings** (*pronounced 'dih-lin-ee-eight'*) from the Latin, *delineare*: to outline, from *de-*: out + *lineare*: to line, from *linea*: line

e.g. In his book *The Audacity of Hope*, Obama **delineates** his vision for the United States of America

to deliquesce (verb) = **to disappear as if by melting; to melt away (as part of the decaying process)** (*pronounced 'de-li-kwes'*) from the Latin, *deliquescere*: to dissolve, from *de-*: down + *liquescere*: to become liquid

e.g. I love the sensation of pan-fried foie gras **deliquescing** on my tongue

denuded of (something) (set phrase) = **to be stripped of (a possession)** *(pronounced 'dih-nyood')* from the Latin, *denudare*: to strip, from *de-*: completely + *nudare*: to bare

e.g. Now that e-readers are so popular, bookshelves are often entirely **denuded of** books; and in their stead, plants and photo frames stand guard

to deprecate (verb) = **to deplore** *(pronounced 'dep-ri-keight')* from the Latin, *deprecari*: to pray against (as an evil), from *de-*: down + *precari*: to pray

e.g. 'Serious' literary authors tend to **deprecate** books like *The Girl with the Dragon Tattoo* – perhaps out of jealousy that the latter has sold 50 million copies and counting

dereliction of duty (set phrase) = **the deliberate abandoning of one's duty** *('dereliction' is pronounced 'der-uh-lik-shuhn') for full explanation, see box below*

e.g. When he walked out on his pregnant wife, his father-in-law accused him of a **dereliction of duty**

'dereliction of duty' is a specific offence applicable to the US military (under the Code of Laws of the United States). The etymology of the word hints at the nature of the offence: 'dereliction' is from the Latin, 'derelinquere': 'to abandon', ultimately from 'de-': 'completely' + 'relinquere': 'to leave'.

A member of the military guilty of 'dereliction of duty' has either deliberately refused to perform his duty, or has incapacitated himself – owing to excessive alcoholic consumption, for example – to such a degree that he is unable to execute his role.

Bizarrely enough, it was Jimmy Stewart, the actor, who presided over the first court martial where someone was accused of 'dereliction of duty'. (Of course, Stewart was not an actor at that stage, and was only known by his military title, which was 'Colonel James M. Stewart'.) The court martial concerned was held during World War II, and the army officers thus charged were two US Army Air Force lieutenants who had mistakenly dropped bombs on Zürich in Switzerland (which was a neutral country during the war, and therefore ill-deserving of bombs). Eventually – after evidence showing it was the plane's equipment, rather than the officers, at fault – the men were acquitted of the charge. The phrase 'dereliction of duty' has taken on a wider meaning now, and is no longer confined to the military, being suitable for all cases of neglect, military, romantic, or otherwise.

to descant on (a topic) (verb) = **to comment at length about (a topic)** (pronounced '<u>des</u>-kant') from the Latin, *discantus*: a refrain, from *dis-*: apart + *cantus*: song; *'a descant' literally means 'a melodious song'*

e.g. The wedding guests were moved to tears as the groom **descanted on** his love for his bride

desiccated (adj.) = **lacking spirit (originally used of food that has been preserved by removing the moisture from it)** (pronounced '<u>des</u>-i-kay-tid') from the Latin, *desiccare*: to make thoroughly dry

e.g. When you watch *The Godfather*, you find yourself rooting for crime boss Michael Corleone; for, despite his **desiccated** soul, he is the best of a bad bunch

détente (noun) = **the easing of troubled relations** (pronounced: 'day-tonte') from the French, *détente*: loosening

e.g. After Kim Jong Il died suddenly, US diplomats worried the emerging **détente** between Washington and Pyongyang might reverse

dewlap (noun) = **a fold of loose skin hanging from the neck** from the Old English, *dewe lappe*, from *dewe*: of unknown meaning + *lappe*: loose fold; *the word was originally used of cattle, then began to be used of the loose skin of humans too*

e.g. Dewlaps hang down from the chins of old people

diegetic

diegetic (noun) = *(in a film or novel)* **concerning the world as experienced by the characters in the film (who only 'see' the events on screen), as opposed to the world experienced by the audience (who 'see' the events on screen, but who also see, for example, the neighbour in the seat next to them munching his popcorn, whom the characters on screen cannot see)** *(pronounced 'dahy-uh-jet-ik')* for full explanation, see box below

e.g. Her husband, who was sitting next to her in the cinema, was laughing so loudly that she couldn't hear the **diegetic** sounds coming from the screen

---

'diegetic' is the adjectival form of 'diegesis', which comes from the Greek, 'diegesis': 'a narrative', and ultimately from 'dia-': 'across' + 'hegeisthai': 'to guide'. It was the Greek philosopher Plato (424–348 BC) who invented the term 'diegesis' (but it's best not to go into exactly what Plato meant by 'diegesis' as it's the exact opposite to what we mean today by the word).

We use 'diegetic' nowadays to refer to the world as experienced by the characters in the film (who only 'see' the events on screen), as opposed to the world as experienced by the audience (who 'see' the events on screen, but also the neighbour in the seat next to them picking his nose, whom the characters on screen cannot see).

A good way to show this difference is to consider the music in a film. If a character on screen turns up the volume of his car radio, and his on-screen wife objects, then this radio song – which is clearly being heard by the fictional characters, and is therefore part of the fictional world presented – is labelled 'diegetic'. However, if that same husband and wife later run together along a beach, over which a soundtrack of 'She Loves Me' has been superimposed by the director, then this soundtrack music – which the audience can hear, but which the on screen husband and wife can't (as far as they're concerned, the beach they're running along, is a silent one) – is 'non-diegetic'.

---

diffuse (adj.) = *(of a speaker)* **rambling; OR** *(of concept)* **widely dispersed** *(pronounced: 'dih-fyoos')* from the Latin, *diffundere*: to pour out, from *dis-*: away, + *fus-*, the past participle stem of *fundere*: to pour; *'diffuse' literally means 'poured out and caused to spread' (hence 'rambling', of speech)*

e.g. The priest's sermon was **diffuse**, so the congregation couldn't concentrate and soon fell asleep

to dilate on (a topic) (verb) = **to speak or write at length about (a topic)** *(pronounced 'dahy-leight')* from the Latin, *dilatare*: to enlarge, from *di-*: apart + *latus*: wide; *a 'dilation' during a pregnancy refers of course to 'a widening' or 'enlargening', and 'to dilate on a topic' is, similarly, to 'enlarge on a topic'*

e.g. In their Oscar acceptance speech, actors usually **dilate on** their gratitude to their agent

diorama (noun) = **a three-dimensional scene in which figures are arranged against a background** *(pronounced 'dee-uh-ram-uh')* from the Greek, *dia-*: through + *horama*: view *(just as 'panorama' means 'all of a view' in Greek)*

e.g. Some people love to collect snow globes: those tiny glass balls with **dioramas** of Alpine scenes inside, over which snowflakes fall (if you shake the globe)

to disavow (something) (noun) = **to reject (something)** from the Old French, *desavouer*: to disavow

e.g. If a politician makes a racist comment, his words will quickly be **disavowed** by the party leader

disconsolate (adj.) = **cheerless** *(pronounced 'dis-kon-suh-lit')* from the medieval Latin, *disconsolatus*, from *dis-* (expressing a reversal) + *consolatus*: consoled, past participle of *consolari*: to console

e.g. After one spouse dies, the one left alive is often **disconsolate**

dirigiste (adj.) = **(of an economy) strongly influenced by the government, rather than left alone to free-market forces** *(pronounced 'dir-ig-iste')* from the Latin, *dirigere*: to direct

e.g. The United States has historically responded to a weak economy by announcing new building projects to boost employment: a typical manoeuvre for a **dirigiste** economy

discommodious (adj.) = **causing trouble** *(pronounced 'dis-kuh-mohd-ius')* from the French, *dis-*: not + *commode*: convenient

e.g. On a hot day, an overcoat is somewhat **discommodious**

47

discursive (adj.) = *(of speech or writing)* **tending to depart from the main point and thus cover a range of subjects** from the Latin, *discurrere*: to run away, from *dis-*: away + *currere*: to run

e.g. When alcohol flows, conversation becomes more **discursive**

to disgorge (an object) (verb) = **to discharge violently (an object), as if from the throat** *(pronounced 'dis-gorj')* from the French, *desgorgier*: to pour out, from *des-*: expressing removal, + *gorge*: throat

e.g. The plane landed with a sudden thump, before **disgorging** its fraught-looking passengers

disinformation (noun) = **false information, intended to mislead** based on the Russian, *dezinformatsiya*: misinformation

e.g. Liberal politicians accuse Fox TV of spreading **disinformation** harmful to the left

disinterested (adj.) = *(regarding a situation)* **having no axe to grind in a particular situation** from the English words, *dis-* + *interest*

e.g. The only way bankers can become truly **disinterested** is if their personal remuneration is not tied to the profits they generate

disputatious (adj.) = *(of a person)* **fond of heated arguments** *(pronounced 'dis-pyoo-tey-shuhs')* from the Latin, *disputare*: to dispute, from *dis-*: apart + *putare*: to reckon

e.g. Shakespeare's *Much Ado about Nothing* features Beatrice and Benedick, two **disputatious** lovers involved in the 'merry war of wit'

dissonance between (one thing) and (another thing) (set phrase) = **a lack of agreement between (one thing) and (another thing)** from the Latin, *dissonare*: to not agree in sound

e.g. There had long been a **dissonance between** his idea of a pleasant afternoon (which involved fishing) **and** that of his wife (which revolved around shopping)

distrait (adj.) = *(of a person)* **absent-minded because of anxiety** *(pronounced 'dih-strey')* from the French, *destrait*, ultimately from the Latin, *distrahere*: to pull apart

e.g. The stress of conducting an affair was making him **distrait** and his job was suffering as a result

diurnal (adj.) = **of, or during, daytime** *(pronounced 'dahy-ur-nal')* from the Latin, *diurnus*: daily

e.g. Vampires are nocturnal but humans are mainly **diurnal**

divagations (noun) = **digressions** *(pronounced 'dahy-vuh-gey-shuns')* from the Latin, *divagari*: to wander around, from *di-*: widely + *vagari*: to wander

e.g. The interviewer looked on, perplexed, as John Lennon embarked on one of his drug-fuelled **divagations**

docent (noun) = **a sort of teacher: usually a tour guide at a museum, or a lecturer at a university museum** *(pronounced 'doh-suhnt')* from the Latin, *docere*: to teach

e.g. When you're looking around a museum in a group, your mind sometimes wanders as it's impossible to stay focused on what the **docent** is saying for 100 per cent of the time

(the) dog days of summer (set phrase) = **the hottest days of the summer (that occur between July and September)** *for full explanation, see box below*

e.g. It's when the days are cold – rather than during **the dog days of summer** – that people turn up their Aga ovens

---

'dog days' is a translation of the Latin, 'dies caniculares', meaning 'dog star days'.

'dog star days' was the Roman description for the hot weather between early July and early September, so called because the Romans falsely believed this summer heat could be explained by the 'dog star' (known as 'Sirius' today) rising and setting with the sun during these months. (And the reason for the 'dog star' being called thus, is that it's the brightest star in the constellation known as 'Greater Dog', or 'Canis Major'.)

And, as July to September is the hottest period of the year – and hence, the most sluggish – the phrase 'dog days' has the connotation of a period of inactivity.

doggerel (noun) = **appalling poetry** (*pronounced 'dog-er-el'*) from the Middle English, *doggerel*, apparently from *dog* (as the poetry is so bad that it is only fit for dogs) + *-rel*

e.g. Sir John Betjeman – author of the poem 'Slough', which starts 'Come friendly bombs and fall on Slough! / It isn't fit for humans now...' – was incapable of writing **doggerel**

doltish (adj.) = **stupid** from the English, *dolt*, a variant of *dulled*, past participle of *dull*

e.g. During half-time in football matches, the nation is forced to listen to the **doltish** commentary of the TV pundits

doppelgänger (noun) = **a double of a person** (*pronounced 'dop-uhl-geng-er'*) from the German, **doppelgänger**: double-goer

e.g. My aunt has ravishing brown hair and an attractive facial mole: some say she is Cindy Crawford's **doppelgänger**

E

ectoplasm (noun) = **a wispy cloud** (*pronounced 'ek-tuh-plaz-uhm'*) from the Greek, *ektos*: outside + *plasma*: something moulded; *an 'ectoplasm' originally referred – in the 19th century – to a supernatural substance that allegedly rose up, out of the body of a medium during a séance, and then went on to take the shape of a spirit*

e.g. When you exhale a cigarette in the sun, the smoke turns straight into **ectoplasm** in the light

Eeyorish (adj.) = **gloomy (the direct opposite of Tiggerish, see later entry)** (*pronounced 'ee-or-ish'*) from Eeyore, the old grey donkey in Winnie the Pooh (1926) by A.A. Milne; Eeyore was marked by his gloomy outlook, living in an area labelled on the map in The House at Pooh Corner as 'Eeyore's Gloomy Place: Rather Boggy and Sad'

e.g. Many comedians who are upbeat in public are in fact **Eeyorish** in private

efflorescence (noun) = **blossoming** (*pronounced 'ef-luh-res-uhns'*) from the Latin, *efflorescere*: to blossom, from *e-*: out + *florescere*: to begin to bloom, from *flos, flor-*: a flower

e.g. She wore glasses and braces during her teenage years: but when she hit 20, she removed both items, and many commented on the overnight **efflorescence** of her beauty

eidolon (noun) = **an apparition of a person** (pronounced *'ahy-doh-lun'*) from the Greek, *eidos*: form; *in ancient Greek literature (such as the* Odyssey*), eidolons appear after death, as ghostly lookalikes of a dead human*

e.g. Whilst tidying, she stumbled across an old love letter from her first boyfriend, and, reading it, she recalled with amusement her 17-year-old **eidolon**

eleemosynary (adj.) = **relating to charity** (*pronounced 'el-uh-mos-uh-ner-ee'*) from the Latin, *eleemosyna*: alms, from the Greek, *eleemosune*: compassion

e.g. Centuries of Christianity have ensured an **eleemosynary** impulse is ingrained in us

---

Elysium (noun) = **a place of complete bliss** (*pronounced 'ih-lizh-ee-uhm'*) from the Greek, *Elusion* (*pedion*): (plain) of the blessed; *in Greek mythology, 'Elysium' was the equivalent of the Christian heaven*

e.g. For tennis lovers, Wimbledon is **Elysium**

embrocation (noun) = **a liquid rubbed into the skin to relieve pain** (*pronounced 'em-broh-kay-shuhn'*) from the Greek, *embrokhe*: lotion

e.g. His wife's compliments were an essential **embrocation** for his ego

emeritus (*adj. that can go before, or after, the noun*) = **(of a person) retired but retaining an honorary title equivalent to that held immediately before retirement** (*pronounced 'ih-mer-i-tuhs'*) from the Latin, past participle of *emereri*: to earn one's discharge by service, from *e-*: out + *mereri*: to earn

e.g. In his memoir *Don't Mind if I Do*, Hollywood playboy **emeritus** George Hamilton – now well into his seventies – reviewed his life and loves

emissary (noun) = **someone who has been sent on a special mission** (*pronounced 'em-uh-ser-ee'*) from the Latin, *emissarius*: scout, from *emittere*: to send out

e.g. On her wedding day, clad in radiant white, Grace Kelly looked like an **emissary** from a finer world

emollient (adj.) = **(of someone's manner) soothing** (*pronounced 'ih-mol-yuhnt'*) from the Latin, *emollire*: to make soft, from *e-*: out + *mollis*: soft

e.g. Obama decided to avoid using phrases like 'axis of evil', and instead referred to other countries in more **emollient** tones

to emote (verb) = **(of a person) to display emotions openly** (*pronounced 'ih-moht'*) *from the early 20th century, a back formation from 'emotion'*

e.g. Over the last decade, it has become the norm for politicians to **emote** during TV interviews

(the) empyrean (noun) = **the heavens** (*pronounced 'em-pir-ee-uhn'*) from the Greek, *empurious*: from heaven, from *en-*: in + *pur*: fire (*because the ancient Greeks believed heaven was a realm of pure fire*)

e.g. The aeroplane rose into the **empyrean** and disappeared from sight

(an) encomium (to someone / something) (noun) = **a tribute (to someone / something)** (*pronounced 'en-koh-mee-uhm'*) from the Greek, *enkomion*: eulogy, from *en-*: within + *komos*: revel

e.g. After the wedding dinner was over, the groom delivered a gushing **encomium** to his wife

endogenous (adj.) = **having an internal cause** (*as opposed to exogenous: having an external cause*) (*pronounced 'en-doj-uh-nuhs'*) *'endogenous' derives from the Greek, 'endo-': 'within' + '-genous': 'producing'; whereas 'exogenous' is from the Greek 'exo-': 'outside' + '-genous'*

e.g. Sometimes an aeroplane's engine failure is **exogenous** (such as when geese fly into the engine, disrupting it); and sometimes, a plane falls out of the sky for **endogenous** reasons (such as when a wire inside the engine snaps owing to wear and tear)

enormity (noun) = **a grave crime;** *note that, to convey vast size, the correct word is 'enormousness'* from the Latin, *'enormitas'*, from *'e-'*: 'out of' + *'norma'*: 'standard'; thus 'enormity' literally means 'deviation from (moral) standards'

e.g. Hitler's murder of the Jews was an **enormity** beyond belief

entente (noun) = **a friendly understanding between different factions** (*pronounced 'ahn-tahnt'*) from the French, *entente (cordiale)*: (friendly) understanding

e.g. Nadal and Federer may be intense rivals on court; but it's clear from interviews off court that they enjoy an **entente**

entropy (noun) = *(of a society left to itself)* **a gradual decline into mayhem** *(pronounced 'en-truh-pee') for full explanation, see box below*

e.g. Believers argue that, if religion disappears, **entropy** will result

---

'entropy' derives from the Greek, 'en-': 'inside' + 'trope': 'transformation'. In physics, 'entropy' is the tendency towards 'equilibrium', or 'sameness', within a situation, i.e. hotter areas of a system will, with time, lose heat, while cooler areas will get warmer; in the same way, organisms which are now alive, will die; and the universe, which is now hot, will eventually cool down (a process that has already started). The classic example of entropy in action is that of cold ice melting in your (slightly warmer) gin and tonic.

In other words, because 'entropy' determines that thermal energy always flows spontaneously from regions of higher temperature to regions of lower temperature (in the form of heat), it can be said that 'entropy' changes the 'order' of the initial systems (from one patch of hot and one patch of cold, into one larger area of exactly the same temperature), and, therefore, that 'entropy' is an expression of 'disorder' (as the initial 'order' has been changed). Hence 'entropy' gradually acquired its metaphorical meaning, when applied to society as a whole, of 'a gradual descent into disorder'. The facts are bleak: entropy – like time – runs in one direction only, and you cannot turn back the clock on the process.

One of Sir Tom Stoppard's most lauded plays, Arcadia (1993), is partially about 'entropy': in it, one character explains that her steam engine operates under the principle of 'entropy' (in this case, of heat transference, as cold water is turned into hot steam); and that the universe itself does too – for the universe is also changing states and winding down.

---

epicene (adj.) = **effeminate** *(pronounced 'ep-i-seen')* from the Greek, *epikoinos*, from *koinos*: common

e.g. Starved male models on the catwalk all sport the same **epicene** look

epigone (noun) = **an inferior imitator** (*pronounced 'ep-i-gohne'*) from the Greek, *epugonoi*: those born afterwards

e.g. Critics of David Cameron say he is merely the 'heir to Blair': nothing more than an **epigone** of Tony

epistemological (adj.) = **relating to the study of knowledge (specifically what distinguishes warranted belief from mere opinion)** (*pronounced 'ih-pis-tuh-muh-loj-i-kuhl'*) from the Greek, *epistasthai*: to know how to do

e.g. Imagine if newspaper editors stopped checking their facts: the public would be plunged into an **epistemological** nightmare

errant (adj.) = **straying from the proper course** (*pronounced 'er-uhnt'*) from the Latin, *errant-*: erring, ultimately from *iterare*: to go on a journey, from *iter*: journey

e.g. After the dust had settled on the financial crisis, the witchhunt began for the **errant** bankers responsible

eschatological (adj.) = **concerning death and judgement day** (*pronounced 'es-kah-tol-uh-ji-kal'*) from the Greek, *eskhatos*: last, extreme

e.g. It's a waste of time to discuss **eschatological** matters, say militant atheists, who are 100 per cent convinced there is no life after death

esprit de corps (noun) = **(of a group) a shared spirit of comradeship** (*pronounced 'e-spree duh kawr'*) from the French, *esprit de corps*: spirit of the body

e.g. When it became clear that Gadaffi's regime was foundering, the **esprit de corps** amongst his supporters evaporated

55

esprit de l'escalier (noun) = **the feeling you get when the perfect riposte comes to you too late** (*pronounced 'e-spree des-kal-i-ey'*) *for full explanation, see box below*

e.g. Hours after the TV debate with Obama had ended, Romney's **esprit de l'escalier** kicked in, and he realised exactly what he should have said

---

The phrase derives from the French expression, 'l'esprit de l'escalier', meaning 'staircase wit'. It was French philosopher Denis Diderot (1713–84) who invented the term during a description of a dinner party. (Diderot is the French philosopher best known for his work Encyclopaedia or a Systematic Dictionary of the Sciences, Arts and Crafts, *which sets down in one book the work of scientists and intellectuals during the Enlightenment, as they sought to combat superstition.) During this dinner at the home of a wealthy politician, a remark was directed to Diderot which rendered him dumbfounded because, he explains,*

'...a sensitive man, such as myself, knocked sideways by the argument levelled against him, becomes confused and can only think clearly once more, when he gets to the bottom of the staircase.'

In the house Diderot was referring to in the above quotation, the dining room was located on the first floor, so that to have reached – in Diderot's words – 'the bottom of the staircase' (or 'l'escalier' in French) means you were on your way out of the house: at this stage, the dinner party was definitively over, and any retort that occurred to you then, had come to you too late to be useful in the argument (that was now over). Today, 'esprit de l'escalier' continues to refer to the feeling of any such comebacks that strike you long after an argument has come to an end.

---

etiology (noun) = *(of a disease or problem)* **the cause** (*pronounced 'ee-tee-ol-uh-jee'*) from the Greek, *aitiologia*, from *aitia*: a cause + -*logia*: a speaking

e.g. His troubled childhood was almost certainly the **etiology** of his alcoholism

ex ante (set phrase) = *(of the expected results of a future event)* **predicted before the event in question takes place** (*pronounced* *'eks an-tee')* from the Latin, *ex ante*: before the event

e.g. Government officials predict the effect of tax rises **ex ante** – rather than just going ahead and implementing rises, to see what happens – so as to know in advance how much extra revenue they can expect to earn from the increase

ex post (set phrase) = *(of the expected results of a future event)* **predicted based on extrapolating from past occurrences** *(pronounced 'eks pohst')* from the Latin, *ex post*: after the fact

e.g. After the financial crisis, banks realised that the traditional way of working out their maxium losses – which involved using **ex-post** markets data to forecast future losses – was wrong, as this method failed everyone in 2008

excrescence (noun) = **an outgrowth** *(pronounced 'iks-kres-uhns')* from the Latin, *excrescentia*: an outgrowth, from *excrescere*: to grow out, from *ex-*: out + *crescere*: to grow; *'excrescence' literally refers – in medical terminology – to an abnormal outgrowth on the body, such as a wart*

e.g. The public views the average banker as an **excrescence** on the body of capitalism

exegesis (noun) = **an analysis** *(pronounced 'ek-si-jee-sis')* from the Greek, *exegeisthai*: to interpret, from *ex-*: out + *hegeisthai*: to guide

e.g. James Joyce's *Ulysses* is not the sort of book you can hope to understand first time around, for it requires considerable **exegesis**

exigencies (pl. noun) = **urgent requirements** *(pronounced 'ek-si-juhn-sees')* from the Latin, *exigentia*: a demand, from *exigere*: to enforce, from *ex-*: thoroughly + *agere*: to perform

e.g. He was married to a manic depressive, and the **exigencies** of supporting his wife meant his work life was beginning to suffer

exiguous (adj.) = **very small in size** *(pronounced 'i-zig-yoo-uhs')* from the Latin, *exiguus*: scanty, from *exigere*: to weigh exactly

e.g. Celebrity magazines are teeming with photos of actresses on beaches, wearing **exiguous** bikinis

expectoration (noun) = *(of words or mucus)* **that which has been discharged from your chest** *(pronounced 'ik-spek-tuh-rey-shuhn')* from the Latin, *expectorare*: to expel from the chest, from *ex-*: out + *pectus*: the breast

e.g. The letter that the serial killer sent to the police was bursting with his twisted **expectorations**

to explicate (a concept) (verb) = **to explain (a concept)** from the Latin, *explicare*: to unfold, from *ex-*: out + *plicare*: to fold

e.g. If a US President is accused of adultery, he will – guilty or not – rapidly hold a press conference to **explicate** the situation

to extenuate (a crime or bad situation) (verb) = **to lessen (a crime or bad situation)** from the Latin, *extenuare*: to make small, from *ex-*: out + *tenuare*: to make thin, based on *tenuis*: thin

e.g. To **extenuate** her grief, her friend came around with a basket of muffins

to have an eye on the main chance (set phrase) = **to be constantly looking for an opportunity to make money** *'The main chance' is a phrase that was invented in 1579 by John Luly in his book* Eupheus, the Anatomy of Wyt, *as a way of referring to 'the best chance for financial gain'*

e.g. Richard Branson made his billions by having **an eye on the main chance**

eyrie (noun) = **a high-up place** *(pronounced 'air-ee')* from the Latin, *area*: nest of a bird of prey; *an eyrie literally refers to the nest of an eagle high up in a tree*

e.g. Many people dream of going to Paris, renting some Left Bank **eyrie** and finally writing that novel

Fabian tactics (set phrase) = *(of a battle strategy)* **wearing out an opponent by strategies such as delay and evasion – rather than by direct confrontation** *(as exemplified by Fabius, a Roman general)* (pronounced '<u>fey</u>-bee-uhn') for full explanation, see box below

e.g. Rather than tiring out his opponent with **Fabian** tactics, Mike Tyson often went for the knock-out punch

---

The phrase 'Fabian tactics' derives from the name of a renowned Roman general, called 'Quintus Fabius Maximus Verrucosus' (280–203 BC), who was also known as 'Fabius the Delayer' ('Fabius Cunctator').

After the military genius Hannibal – leader of Carthage (now Tunisia in North Africa) – defeated the Roman army at Cannae in 216 BC, Fabius prevented Hannibal's hordes from conquering Rome by wearing down the invaders with a series of tactics, rather than by confronting them directly in battle. Hannibal was in a strange land with a large army that had to be nourished, and without any aid from outside; so Fabian, knowing he'd lose any direct scrap with Hannibal, instead attacked the troops Hannibal had send out to scavenge for food, weakening his foe this way.

Some of his own side saw this behaviour of Fabius's as being cowardly and he was replaced with another general who was prepared to engage Hannibal directly in battle. But – just as Fabius had foreseen – this resulted in huge losses for Rome; and soon Fabius was reinstalled as leader. For the rest of the war, Fabius's tactics were followed and Rome was saved. Suddenly Fabius's sobriquet of 'Cunctator' ('the delayer'), which had been given to him in mockery, assumed a mantle of respectability. Today, anyone who uses delaying tactics in any battle – military or metaphorical – can be said to be employing 'Fabian tactics'. (One famous modern-day proponent is 'The Fabian Society', a think tank that, within the battlefield of political ideologies, advocates the gradual, and thus, Fabius-style adoption of socialism – as opposed to the revolutionary, overnight implementation of socialism advocated by Marxists and Trotskyists.)

59

fandango (noun) = **silly nonsense** *(pronounced 'fan-dang-go') for full explanation, see box below*

e.g. Kate and William's holidays abroad are accompanied by the usual **fandango** of paparazzi and photographers

---

A 'fandango' is an elaborate Spanish dance originating in the 18th century; the Spanish 'fandango' derives from the Portuguese 'fado', meaning 'sad song'.

This courtship dance is performed by a couple who move together closely and provocatively. Traditionally, their dancing is accompanied by hand-clapping, guitars and tambourines.

Overall, the effect is quite extravagant – and, to some people, doubtless a bit over the top; hence the word 'fandango' at some point assumed its current metaphorical significance of 'silly nonsense'.

---

farrago (noun) = **a hodgepodge** *(pronounced 'fuh-rah-go')* from the Latin, *farrago*: mix of grains (to feed animals), from *far*: corn

e.g. Their divorce started off amicably, but soon become a **farrago** of accusation and counter-accusation

Fauvist (adj.) = *(of a painting)* **containing simple shapes and exaggerated colours** *(pronounced 'fohv-ist') for full explanation, see box below*

e.g. As we went around the exhibition, my date described the paintings – which consisted of a few squiggles against a bright red and blue backdrop – as **Fauvist**

'Fauvist' is a good one to know when you're touring an art gallery and trying to impress a member of the opposite sex: you can use it of just about any painting which contains exaggerated colours, and simple shapes (usually with clear, black contours around them).

As a movement, 'Fauvism' was founded by Henri Matisse in Paris, and only lasted from 1904–8, and – like so many movements – it was largely a reaction to a previous one: in this case, Impressionism, which focused on very realistic, true-to-life (and certainly not exaggerated) renditions of shapes and colours (with Monet and Manet being perhaps the most prominent exponents of Impressionism).

The term 'Fauvist' derives from the French, 'fauve': 'a wild beast'. This was because of an incident in 1905 at a gallery featuring Matisse's work, when a famous French art critic exclaimed, of a plain Renaissance-type statue in the midst of the very un-plain, colourful works by Matisse, 'Donatello au milieu des fauves!' (which means, 'Donatello among the wild beasts!'). The phraseology of this insult – which likened Matisse's works to the 'wild beasts' (or 'fauves') – stuck, and Matisse's movement became known as 'Fauvist'.

favela (noun) = **a slum** *(pronounced 'fah-ve-lah')* from the Portuguese, *favela*: a Brazilian shanty town

e.g. The city of Rome is allegedly now so lawless that it resembles one giant **favela**, where shoot-outs are commonplace

fealty (to) (noun) = *(of a subordinate)* **loyalty (to)** *(as sworn to a lord by a 'vassal', see 'vassal' later on)* *(pronounced 'fee-uhl-tee')* from the Old French, *fealte*, from the Latin, *fidelitas*: faithfulness

e.g. Democrats have long suspected the Republicans of **fealty to** oil barons

federalism (noun) = *(of government)* **a central authority presiding over self-governing units** from the Latin, *foedus, foederis*: covenant, from *fides*: faith

e.g. Some commentators have suggested **federalism** as a solution to the European crisis, with a German-controlled hub overseeing all the other countries

to have feet of clay

to have feet of clay (set phrase) = *(of a person in high station)* **to have a character flaw** *for full explanation, see box below*

e.g. After the Monica Lewinsky scandal, some whispered that then-President, Bill Clinton, had **feet of clay**

The phrase 'feet of clay' originates from the Bible – specifically, from the Book of Daniel.

In this book, King Nebuchadnezzar of Babylon (modern-day Iraq) experiences a terrifying dream in which he envisages a huge metal statue that is composed entirely of strong metal – except for its feet, which are 'partially clay'. The brittle, 'clay' element of these feet makes Nebuchadnezzar realise the statue is vulnerable and will, one day, fall; and indeed, as the dream unfolds, a massive stone strikes the statue at its feet, and it smashes to smithereens.

Once awake, King Nebuchadnezzar reacts to this dream by calling together his court: unless they can explain what his dream means, the king wil have his mystic interpreters executed. Hearing this, the prophet Daniel seeks divine inspiration, then delivers his verdict: the dream means that King Nebuchadnezzar's kingdom is – like the statue in the dream – in danger of destruction, but by unforeseen opponents (represented by the stone in the dream). Nebuchadnezzar agrees with Daniel's interpretation, and Daniel's reward is to become chief governor of Babylon. The phrase 'feet of clay' persists today, to describe someone who – like the statue in the king's dream – has a fundamental flaw after all.

---

feint (noun) = **a feigned appearance** *(pronounced 'faint')* from the French, *feindre*: to feign; *a 'feint' literally means 'that which is feigned' and originally referred to a pretend thrust in fencing*

e.g. His air of nonchalance was a **feint** to conceal his overwhelming ardour for her

fiat money (set phrase) = **paper money issued by a government – but which cannot be converted into something real, like gold** *('fiat' is pronounced 'fee-aht') for full explanation, see box below*

e.g. When you realise that the note in your wallet is merely **fiat money** – and can never be exchanged for something real like gold – then money seems an illusion

The phrase 'fiat money' comes from the Latin, 'fiat': 'let it be done', from 'fieri': 'to be done'. 'Fiat money' has no intrinsic value (i.e. it cannot be converted into gold): in fact, the only reason it is worth anything at all is as a result of a government law (which is also called a 'fiat'). 'Fiat money' originated in 11th-century China; in modern times, since 1971 all major world currencies have been 'fiat money'.

To take the example of the United States (still the world's biggest economy), between 1944 and 1971, the dollar was directly convertible to a fixed amount of gold (as a result of an agreement signed by all 44 Allied nations, whose currencies were then all tied to the dollar to ensure global stability after the war). This was all great, until the early 1970s, when the United States – crippled by the cost of the Vietnam War (1955–75) – started to print more dollars as a way out of its economic difficulties.

Concerned by the resulting inflation emanating from the United States, the other Allied nations gradually dropped out of the accord signed in 1944 (with inflation-wary West Germany being the first member to unilaterally leave). Then, to put a stop to this inflation – that was making the cost of goods unpalatable to so many around the world (because every country's currency was inflating higher alongside the dollar) – on 15 August 1971, the United States unilaterally terminated convertibility of the dollar to gold. With one stroke, 'the Breton Woods system' (the name for the agreement signed in 1944) was at an end – and the dollar had, overnight, become 'fiat money'. (Incidentally, since President Nixon made this decision without consulting other countries, the international community informally named this episode 'the Nixon shock'.)

to filibuster

to filibuster (verb) = *(of politicians)* **to use delaying tactics – especially long, irrelevant speeches – to delay progress in making certain laws** *(pronounced 'fil-uh-buhs-ter') for full explanation, see box below*

e.g. Any attempts by the Democrats to limit gun ownership are often derailed by Republican **filibustering**

'to filibuster' derives from the Spanish 'filibustero', used to describe 16th-century pirates who pillaged Spanish colonies in the West Indies; by 1850, the noun had evolved to describe the tactics of those who 'pirated' debate in the US Senate.

'filibustering' has a long tradition: one of the earliest known practitioners of 'the filibuster' was the Roman senator Cato the Younger (95–46 BC). If he opposed a legislation, Cato would often obstruct the surrounding debate by speaking non-stop until nightfall. As the Roman Senate required all business to conclude by dusk, Cato's purposefully long-winded speeches were an effective device to delay a vote.

Modern day examples are rife. For example, in the United Kingdom, on Friday 20 April 2007, a bill – aimed at making politicians immune from 'The Freedom of Information Act' (which is designed to allow the public 'right of access' to information held by public authorities) – was 'filibustered' by a collection of MPs, led by Liberal Democrats Simon Hughes and Norman Baker, who debated for five hours non-stop, thereby ensuring time ran out for that particular parliamentary day (and that the bill was postponed until another day).

---

filigree (noun) = **an intricate branching pattern *(often in gold ornamentation)*** *(pronounced 'fil-i-gree')* from the Italian, *filigrana*, from the Latin, *filum*: thread + *granum*: seed

e.g. I got out of the sea and lay in the sun; and after a while, I noticed on my arm a white **filigree** of dried sea salt

fin de siècle (set phrase) = *(of a situation)* **decadent, set against the backdrop of an approaching end** *(pronounced 'fahn duh see-ek-luh') for full explanation, see box below*

e.g. Knowing he was days away from leaving office, the President commissioned a 'no expenses spared' party in the White House, reflecting the '**fin de siècle**' atmosphere in the building

---

The expression 'fin de siècle' is the French for 'end of the century'. It originally referred to the closing years of the 19th century in France, regarded as a time for breaking free from traditional social and moral norms. These closing years were also part of 'La Belle Époque' (1890–1914), an immensely fertile period marked by the creation of The Eiffel Tower, the automobile, the discovery of both Matisse and Picasso and the perfecting of the drink champagne.

These final few years of the 19th century were characterised both by despair (at the ending of one century), but also by hope (at the beginning of another): feelings exasperated by the knowledge that the best part of a culturally vibrant period ('La Belle Époque') had passed. The other emotions prominent in France at this time – which remain common to the atmosphere of any 'fin-de-siècle' period – were: boredom, cynicism and despair – that such negative emotions should be the result of the previous years of such cultural achievement.

In a broader sense, the expression 'fin de siècle' is now used to characterise any time period that has an ominous mixture of extravagance and decadence, combined with the backdrop of some approaching 'end'. (But the main thing to note is that 'fin de siècle' refers not to the end itself but to the feeling of anticipating this finale.)

---

firmament (noun) = **the heavens** from the Latin, *firmamentum*: a support, from *firmus*: firm, a translation of the Hebrew (in the Old Testament), *raqia*: the roof of the heavens (and also the floor of the earth)

e.g. Bob Dylan is widely acknowledged as one of the great stars in the music **firmament**

flashpoint (noun) = *(metaphorical in meaning)* **a hotspot** from the words *flash* + *point*

e.g. The Middle East has long been a **flashpoint** for conflict

flotsam and jetsam (set phrase) = **a collection of objects or people of little importance** (pronounced '<u>flot</u>-suhm' and '<u>jet</u>-suhm') *for full explanation, see box below*

e.g. Some art critics describe today's artists as charlatans, objecting to their collecting the **flotsam and jetsam** of life, throwing it together and giving it a pseudo-intellectual title like 'archipelago'

'flotsam' and 'jetsam' are both terms used of goods discharged from a ship.

In the case of 'flotsam', the goods have been discharged by accident owing to a shipwreck. ('Flotsam' derives from the Anglo–Norman French, 'floteson', ultimately from the verb 'floter': 'to float'.) 'Jetsam', though, refers to those goods that have been intentionally discharged from the ship – to lighten the vessel (which has turned out to be too heavy and is thus in distress). 'Jetsam' – which literally means 'the object that has been thrown overboard' – derives from the Old French 'getaison': 'a throwing', which later became 'jettison', or 'the act of throwing overboard'. (Incidentally, the other difference between the two, is that, being heavy, 'jetsam' sinks, whereas 'flotsam' floats.)

Today the phrase 'flotsam and jetsam' is used to refer to any collection of discarded odds and ends.

---

flyblown (adj.) = *(literally or metaporically)* **tainted** from the verb, *to flyblow*: to contaminate, especially with the eggs of the blowfly (which then turn into maggots)

e.g. Critics say Monica Lewinisky's revelations have rendered Bill Clinton's reputation **flyblown**

folly (noun) = **an over-the-top building (that has no purpose other than as an ornament)** from the French, *folie*: madness, from *fol*: foolish (in the sense that a 'folly' is an indulgent, foolish undertaking); *of course, 'folly' has another meaning in English: 'foolishness'*

e.g. To some people's thinking, Big Ben is no more than a glorious **folly**

footling (adj.) = **unimportant** from the 19th-century English verb, *footle*: to idle about, from the Old French, *se foutre*: to care nothing (literally: to copulate with oneself), from *foutre*: to copulate with

e.g. A new government does not concern itself with **footling** details, but in getting the bigger picture right

forebearance (noun) = **patient self-restraint** from the Old English, *forberan*: to bear up against, from *for-* + *beran*: to bear

e.g. To get through childbirth, women have to draw on reserves of **forebearance**

foundling (noun) = **a child who looks so unlike his parents that it is as if he has been deserted by his real parents and 'found' and cared for by strangers (who now claim to be his parents themselves)** from the Middle English, *found* + *-ling* (a diminutive suffix)

e.g. When the couple – who were both dark-haired – had a child with silver hair, their unkind neighbours jokingly speculated that the baby must be a **foundling**

frou-frou (adj.) = **overly elaborate, like 'chi-chi'** *(pronounced 'froo-froo')* from the French, *frou frou*: a 19th-century phrase meant to sound like the rustling an elaborate dress makes as its silk scrapes the floor

e.g. The two housewives met for lunch at a **frou-frou** café called *Belle Amie* that served mainly salads and quiches

frowzy (adj.) = **slovenly** *(pronounced 'frou-zee') deriving from the Old English word 'frowsty', meaning 'having an unpleasant smell', itself deriving from the Old French, 'frouste': 'decayed'*

e.g. I was forced to hold my nose when the **frowzy** tramp came and sat next to me on the park bench

to fructify (verb) = **to bear fruit** *(pronounced 'fruhk-tuh-fahy')* from the Latin, *fructificare*: to produce fruit, from *fructus*: fruit

e.g. He was unmarried but wore a wedding ring to business meetings, in the hope that an impression of responsibility might thus **fructify** in onlookers' eyes

fugitive (adj.) = **fleeting** (pronounced *'fyoo-ji-tiv'*) from the Latin, *fugere*: to flee

e.g. After consuming a bottle of wine, he entertained a **fugitive** idea of phoning his ex-wife, but luckily fell asleep before he could enact this plan

fulsome (adj.) = **excessively flattering; OR full** (pronounced *'fuhl-suhm'*) for full explanation, see box below

e.g. His neighbour was not prone to compliments, but, after tasting the roast chicken, he became positively **fulsome**

'fulsome' derives from the two Middle English words 'full' + 'some'.

The word's sense evolved from meaning 'full' in the 13th century, to 'plump' in the 14th century, then to 'overfed' (1640s), and thus, of language, 'offensive to good taste' (1660s) – just as an 'excessively flattering' statement offends because it is too much.

Since the 1960s, however, it has also been commonly used in its original, 13th-century sense, to mean 'full', such as in the phrase 'the TV cameras offered fulsome coverage of the match'. Some people insist this new, easier-to-remember meaning – which, after all, does hark back to the original meaning from hundreds of years ago – is 'wrong'.

---

fungible (adj.) = **interchangeable** (pronounced *'fuhn-juh-buhl'*) from the medieval Latin, *fungi*: to perform, as in *fungi vice*: to take the place of

e.g. Club owners view football players as **fungible** assets and certainly not as equal business partners

fusillade (noun) = a rapid outburst (pronounced *'fyoo-suh-laid)* from the French, *fusiller*: to shoot, from *fusil* (a musket gun) + *ade*

e.g. At the public enquiry into allegations of phone hacking, Rupert Murdoch was exposed to a **fusillade** of questions from politicians

fustian (adj.) = *(of a speech or writing)* **pompous** *(pronounced 'fuhs-ti-an') for full explanation, see box below*

e.g. At the funeral, the priest didn't talk about the dead man at all, but instead hijacked the occasion to deliver a **fustian** speech about 'community spirit'

'fustian' literally means 'a thick cotton cloth', which was used as padding for pillows in the 12th century. The word derives from the Latin, 'fustaneus', meaning 'cloth from Fostat (a suburb of Cairo where such cloth was manufactured)'.

With time, the word assumed a more metaphorical meaning, and 'fustian' language meant words that were just 'padding' (like the 'padding' that 'fustian' originally provided for the innards of a pillow).

(As an aside, the word 'bombast' is very similar, originally referring, in the 16th century, to 'raw cotton, used as padding', before evolving in meaning in the same way as 'fustian' did, to reference language that is also no more than filling.)

---

gadabout (noun) = **a pleasure-seeker** from the Old English verb, *to gad*: to rove + *about*

e.g. All mothers desire to see their son transformed from a disreputable **gadabout** into a respectable family man

gadfly (noun) = **an annoying person who uses criticism to incite others into action; *a 'gadfly' literally means 'a fly that bites and annoys cows'*** from the obsolete English word, *gad*: goad

e.g. Recently his aunt had turned into a **gadfly**, forever asking him when he was going to get on and have his first child

to gainsay (someone) (verb) = **to speak against (someone)** from the Middle English, *gain-*: against + *say*

e.g. Some men get angry when their wives **gainsay** them in public situations

galère (noun) = **a group of undesirable people** (*pronounced 'gal-air'*) from the French, *galère*: a ship-type galley, from the Greek, *galea*: a galley; *the word's negative connotations derive from the belief – now discredited by historians – that it was convicts that manned these ship-type galleys in ancient Greece*

e.g. The President's advisers were becoming increasingly concerned about the **galère** of suspect businessmen he was regularly lunching with

gambit (noun) = **a ploy** from the Italian, *gambetto*: the act of tripping someone up in wrestling, from *gamba*: leg *(which, incidentally, is also the root for 'gambolling around')*

e.g. A favourite **gambit** of politicians is to blame the financial crisis solely on bankers, rather than admit to their own excessive borrowing on behalf of the country

gamesmanship (noun) = **the use of dubious – but not strictly illegal – tactics to win** *for full explanation, see box below*

e.g. Some Paralympic contestants allegedly stuck needles into their testicles – which resulted in no pain as they were paralysed from the waist down – in order to produce performance-boosting adrenalin in their bodies; journalists wrote articles condemning such **gamesmanship**

'gamesmanship' derives from the words 'games' + '-manship', along the lines of 'sportsmanship'; but, whereas sportsmanship is the idea of playing for the enjoyment of the sport, gamesmanship means playing with the sole intention of winning the game.

The term originates from the self-explanatory title of a humorous book written in 1947 by Stephen Potter, The Theory and Practice of Gamesmanship (or the Art of Winning Games without Actually Cheating). *The main tactic advocated by the book is to go out of your way to break the flow of your opponent's play, such as – during a tennis match – taking a judiciously timed loo break, immediately after a bad patch for your opponent, who's then left to consider his recent shortcomings. This is not illegal, but is not considered gentlemanly.*

Soon the phrase became employed in contexts outside of sport, where someone is intent on winning, at any cost, a business contract, for example, or an electoral mandate.

gamey

gamey (adj.) = *(of language)* **sexually suggestive** *for full explanation, see box below*

e.g. In their songs, rappers often use **gamey** language to describe women

---

The word 'gamey' derives from 'game' + '-y'.

'game' itself is from the Old English 'gamen', meaning 'game, fun', then later, 'wild animals caught for sport'.

The first record of 'gamey', in 1863, referred to the meat of such animals 'tasting strongly' (and you can still use 'gamey' in this way today, to describe pungent meat); but with time, 'gamey' began to be used of language, too, to refer to sexually suggestive words.

---

gamut (of) (noun) = **a complete range (of)** *for full explanation, see box below*

e.g. During the play, the actress expressed the **gamut of** emotion, from depression to elation

---

The word 'gamut' owes its birth to an 11th-century musician and former monk named Guido d'Arezzo, who invented a mnemonic to remember the complete musical scale (the full scale being: ut, re, mi, fa, so, la and si). The mnemonic to allow easy recall of this scale was, in Latin, 'Ut queant laxis resonare fibris Mira gestorum famuli tuorum, Solve polluti labii reatum, Sancte Iohannes' (which means in English, 'That with full voices your servants may be able to sing the wonders of your deeds, purge the sin from their unclean lips, O holy John').

Rodgers and Hammerstein later took these bones of this Latin mnemonic and - after replacing the initial 'ut' for the more sing-able 'do' - produced something a bit catchier, in The Sound of Music *(1959),*

*'Doe, a deer, a female deer
Ray, a drop of golden sun
Me, a name I call myself
Far, a long long way to run
Sew, a needle pulling thread
La, a note to follow sew
Tea, I drink with jam and bread
That will bring us back to doe...'*

Now to go back to the 11th-century version, the six-note scale (ut, re, mi, fa, so, la and si) was represented on a higher and lower staff.

to run the gauntlet of (a particular ordeal)

(A staff, when reading music, refers to the set of five horizontal lines, each representing a different musical pitch). In medieval days, the lower staff was called 'gamma' (the Greek word), and on it was placed the lowest note in the scale, 'ut'. And, with time, the first two words – 'gamma' and 'ut' – became combined into 'gam-ut', as a quick way of referring to the whole range of music. By the 17th century 'gamut' was further generalised to mean an entire range of any kind (not just of music).

to run the gauntlet of (a particular ordeal) (set phrase)
= **to endure an ordeal (of a particular type)** *for full explanation, see box below*

e.g. Bing Crosby steeled himself, before pushing open the door to his house and **running the gauntlet of** photographers waiting outside

The phrase 'to run the gauntlet' originally referred to the military punishment – meted out to badly behaved soldiers – of forcedly running between two rows of fellow soldiers, who rained down blows with sticks onto the miscreant as he went down the middle of the two rows. During this grisly torture, another soldier – armed with a sword – would walk in front of the condemned man, to ensure he could move only very slowly down the line and thus had to bear the full brunt of the blows. If the condemned man was still alive when he reached the end of the gauntlet, then he was simply sent back down again, until death resulted.

Weirdly enough, 'running the gauntlet' was considered an honourable form of dispatch, because a soldier thus condemned could face death 'like a man', standing upright (initially at least) and dying amongst his fellow soldiers (even if it was they who were dispatching him).

The etymology of 'gauntlet' is from the Old English 'gantelope', itself a loan word – acquired during the Thirty Years War (1618–48) – from the Old Swedish, 'gattlopp': 'passageway', from 'gatta': 'lane' + 'lopp': 'course' (because the two rows of soldiers made a passageway, down which the condemned man ran). But in time, the spelling of the Old English 'gantelope' became – for reasons no one has ever been able to fathom – influenced by the Old French, 'gantelet', meaning 'a little glove' (see the next entry, 'to take up the gauntlet'). And, as a result of this strange and unaccountable merger in the spelling, the English word 'gauntlet' now has two completely distinct meanings, which can be confusing.

to throw down / take up the gauntlet

to throw down / take up the gauntlet (set phrase) = **to lay down / accept a challenge** *for full explanation, see box below*

e.g. When she got home and found him drinking at 11am, she **threw down the gauntlet** and started a massive argument

and

e.g. After long discussions with his wife – who was allegedly against the idea at first – Obama decided **to take up the gauntlet** and run for President of the United States of America

---

The English word 'gauntlet' also derives from the Old French, 'gantelet', meaning 'little glove', itself from the Old French, 'gant': 'glove'.

And the phrase 'to take up the gauntlet' originated from the custom in the Middle Ages (1100–1453) of a knight challenging a rival knight to a duel, by 'throwing down' (to the ground) one of his two 'gauntlets': a knight's 'gauntlet' being an armoured glove, with an extended cuff all the way up the forearm (for added protection). Whoever 'took up' this gauntlet was then deemed to have accepted the implicit challenge issued.

---

gelded (adj.) = **weakened** *(pronounced with a strong 'g')* from the Old Norse, *gelda*: castrate, from *geldr*: barren; *'gelded' literally refers to a horse that has 'had the testicles removed'*

e.g. Marriages where the wife earns substantially more than the hubsand have a higher-than-average divorce rate: perhaps because some men feel **gelded** in this situation

gelid (adj.) = **very cold** *(pronounced 'jel-id')* from the Latin, *gelidus*: cold, from *gelu*: cold, frost

e.g. When Osama bin Laden heard of the loss of lives in the September 11th tragedy, he reacted with **gelid** indifference

gemütlich (adj.) = **cozy and homely** *(pronounced 'guh-moot-lik')* from the German, *gemütlich*: cheerful

e.g. A sunbeam was streaming through the hotel window, and I lay down on the bed: all was so **gemütlich** that I forgot all about my imminent business meeting and fell fast asleep

gerontocrat (adj.) = **a ruler who is old** (*pronounced 'jer-uhn-tok-rat'*) from the Greek, *geron, geront-*: an old man + *kratos*: power

e.g. After phone-hacking was alleged at the *News of the World* newspaper, politicians arranged an official inquiry, and interviewed Australian **gerontocrat** Rupert Murdoch

gestalt (noun) = **a situation in which the whole is truly greater than the sum of the parts** (*pronounced 'guh-shtahlt'*) from the German, *gestalt*: form, shape

e.g. More important for a novelist than getting each scene right or making each character convincing, is to take a step back and ensure the story's **gestalt** is as he intended it to be

gethsemane (noun) = **a place of great suffering** (*pronounced 'geth-sem-uh-nee'*) *for full explanation, see box below*

e.g. In his retirement, President Nixon doubtless looked back at the Watergate scandal as his **gethsemane**

'Gethsemane' is a garden at the foot of the Mount of Olives in Jerusalem; the word 'gethsemane' comes from the Hebrew, 'gath-shemen': 'the (olive) oil press'.

In the Bible (Matthew 26), 'Gethsemane' is the place where Jesus went with his disciples after the Last Supper, and where Judas betrayed him, kissing Jesus and thus pointing Jesus out to his eventual captors, who were waiting in the wings.

Therefore, 'gethesmane' was a place of suffering for Jesus, and, when we use the word today, we continue to evoke the sense of somewhere where pain is felt.

---

to gladhand (a stranger) (verb) = *(cynical in tone)* **to be overly friendly (with a stranger) so as to gain an advantage** *this verb started life in 1895 as the phrase 'to give the glad hand to (someone)', meaning 'to extend a welcome to (someone)'; eventually the expression was contracted in 1903, into 'to gladhand'*

e.g. The bank threw a cocktail party and instructed every banker present to **gladhand** their clients and laugh at their jokes

glutinous (adj.) = **sticky** (*pronounced 'gloot-in-uhs'*) from the Old French, *glutineux*: gluey, from the Latin, *gluten*: glue; *'glutinous' literally means 'like glue'*

e.g. On awakening, most people's voices are **glutinous** with sleep

gnostic (adj.) = **relating to knowledge** (*pronounced 'nostik'*) from the Greek, *gnostos*: know, related to *gignoskein*: to know

e.g. John Updike said that readers are driven on to read novels because of '**gnostic** suspense': the expectation by the reader that, by reading on, he will acquire new knowledge about life and living

gobbet (noun) = **a morsel** (*pronounced 'gob-it'*) from the Old French, *gobet*, diminutive of *gobe*: a mouthful, from *gober*: to swallow, of Celtic origin

e.g. The one **gobbet** I gleaned from a one-hour TV programme about exercising was this: just 30 seconds of exercise a day can apparently make a huge difference

golgotha / calvary (noun) = **a terrible ordeal** *for full explanation, see box below*

e.g. For an underprivileged woman who conceives in her teens, the pregnancy is often just the first part of a long **golgotha / calvary**

'golgotha' is from the Aramaic, 'gulgulta', meaning '(place of the) skull'; in the Bible (Matthew 27), 'Golgotha' was a hill near Jerusalem where Jesus was crucified; it was known as 'the place of the skull' because it had the shape of a skull.

'Calvary' was the later, Latin term for exactly the same biblical place (as 'Golgotha'): it derives from the Latin word, 'Calvaria', which is related to the Latin, 'calvus', meaning 'bald': the concept of 'baldness' also conveys the smoothness of shape that the hill must have possessed (bald heads and skulls are both similarly smooth, after all).

Today, we continue to refer to an awful event or period as a 'golgotha' or 'calvary'.

gonzo (adj.) = *(of art, esp. journalism)* having an exaggerated and gritty theme, and with the author himself featuring prominently in the work *for full explanation, see box below*

e.g. Certain tabloid journalists indulge in self-aggrandising **gonzo** reporting

---

'gonzo' derives from the Italian, 'gonzo': 'rude'; the word was first used in 1970 by the editor of The Boston Globe *magazine, to describe the prose of oddball journalist Hunter S. Thompson (1937–2005).*

The manic first-person subjectivity of 'gonzo' journalism was reportedly the result of sheer desperation on Hunter S. Thompson's behalf; about to miss a looming deadline, he started frantically sending unfinished pages (full of first-hand observations) ripped out of his notebook to his magazine editor.

To understand how pro-active a journalist must be, to qualify for the label 'gonzo', consider – as the subject matter for a reporter – the case of a blazing inferno. Unlike a traditional journalist, who might record the scene and the aftermath in a clinical, objective fashion, a 'gonzo' journalist would become intensely involved, and probably get hold of a fire helmet, hose and axe and break into the building to help the firefighters; he could then pen a much more involved piece, recording the singed eyebrows of the firefighters, and what it feels like to have flames licking you for an extended period of time. Finally, he'd give free rein to his own internal feelings about the incident.

(to cut the) Gordian knot

(to cut the) Gordian knot (set phrase) = **to solve a difficult problem easily by cheating, or by 'thinking outside the box'**
('Gordian' is pronounced '<u>gawr</u>-dee-uhn') for full explanation, see box below

e.g. Many US presidents attempted to curb Saddam's behaviour, trying various attempts at diplomacy; in the end, though, Bush **cut the Gordian knot** and simply invaded Iraq

---

'cutting the Gordian knot' derives from the legend that Gordius – King of Gordium (in c. 2000 BC), which was the capital of Phrygia (now modern-day Turkey) – tied a knot that was very intricate, and prophesied that whoever undid it would become the ruler of Asia.

Many people tried and failed to untie the knot over the centuries until Alexander the Great turned up in 333 BC, and undid it by simply cutting through it with a sword. Within 10 years, Alexander did indeed become King of Asia.

---

gorgon (noun) = **a terrifyingly ugly woman** *(pronounced '<u>gawr</u>-guhn') for full explanation, see box below*

e.g. Some women put on make-up every single day of their lives, fearing that without it they'll look like a **gorgon**

'gorgon' comes from the Greek 'gorgon', itself deriving from 'gorgos': 'terrible'.

There were three 'gorgons' of Greek legend: hideous female monsters (who happened to be sisters, named Medusa, Stheno and Euryale) whose hair was made up of writhing snakes, and whose horrifyingly ugly visages caused anyone who looked in their direction, to turn into stone. Because of their fearful countenance, the Ancient Greeks often placed stone images of these 'gorgons' on doors, walls and gravestones, in the hope of warding off evil.

From the 16th century, 'gorgon' assumed its current, metaphorical meaning, denoting 'an absurdly ugly female'.

Götterdämmerung (noun) = (*of people or of an institution in power*) **a complete overthrow** (*pronounced 'got-er-<u>dem</u>-uh-roong'*) *for full explanation, see box below*

e.g. When he stood for re-election, many liberal commentators predicted **Götterdämmerung** for George Bush Junior, but he did in fact win a second term

---

'Götterdämmerung' is a German word, meaning 'the twilight of the gods', and refers to an ancient Norse myth about the destruction of the gods ('Ragnarøkkr' in Norse). The reason that it is 'Götterdämmerung' – a German, rather than a Norse, word – that is now used to reference this myth is that it was German composer Richard Wagner (1813–83), who did the most to popularise this Norse legend about the destruction of the gods, immortalising it in his epic opera The Ring Cycle *(known in German as* Der Ring des Nibelungen *and which is composed of four separate epic operas taking some 15 hours to play in all).*

All four of Wagner's operas are based on the original characters from Norse legend – heroes, gods and monsters – who struggle for control of a magic ring that grants the holder dominion over the entire world (not unlike the ring in Tolkein's Lord of the Rings*). It is to the fourth and final opera in this cycle – the longest of the lot at five hours' duration, and featuring a crowning cataclysm – that Wagner gave the name 'Götterdämmerung'.*

In this final disaster in the opera, there is a great battle between good and evil, where the gods are killed. Odin, for example, was swallowed alive by an evil wolf (hence, the title of Götterdämmerung, meaning 'twilight of the gods'); then various natural disasters swiftly follow, for example the sun turns black, and the world is totally submerged by the sea. But the final note is one of hope, as the world resurfaces – fresh and fertile – and the surviving gods live peacefully together. The globe is then repopulated by two lucky human survivors. Today, 'Götterdämmerung' is still used of a similarly dramatic downfall of those in power who – like the gods in the Norse myth, and in Wagner's opera – experience a reversal of fortune and are overthrown.

---

to grandstand (verb) = *(derogatory in tone)* **to behave dramatically to impress an audience** *for full explanation, see box below*

e.g. As they interviewed Rupert Murdoch about the phone hacking allegations, some of the politicians – knowing the TV cameras were upon them – yielded to the temptation **to grandstand**

'to grandstand' is originally a term from baseball slang. In existence since 1895, the word is a shortened version of 'grandstand player', the phrase for a player whose ostentatious antics appealed to spectators sat in the 'grandstand' (the main seating area of the stadium). Writer M.J. Kelly describes such behaviour in Play Ball *in 1888:*

'It's little things of this sort which makes the "grand stand player". They make impossible catches, and when they get the ball they roll all over the field.'

The above attention-grabbing high jinks on the field find an echo today in the dramatic gestures of those crowd-pleasers – usually politicians or celebrities – who we continue to describe as 'grandstanding'.

(the) gravamen (of a complaint) (noun) = **the nub (of a complaint)** *(pronounced 'gruh-vey-muhn')* from the Latin, *gravamen*: a grievance; from the Latin, *gravare*: to burden, from *gravis*: heavy

e.g. The **gravamen** of her complaint against her husband was his pathological infidelity

gravid with (a feeling) = **full of (a feeling)** *(pronounced 'grav-id')* from the Latin, *gravidus*: pregnant, from *gravis*: heavy; *'gravid' literally means 'pregnant'*

e.g. The scene in most divorce courts is **gravid with** unease

greenhorn (noun) = *(informal in tone)* an **inexperienced person** from the 15th-century English noun, *greenhorn*: a young horned animal, from *green* (in the sense of 'fresh, new') + *horn*; *from 1680, greenhorn was used of people*

e.g. If you're admitted to hospital in August, you're allegedly more likely to die than in any other month – for it is in August that **greenhorn** doctors are unleashed on the wards

groundling (noun) = **an uncultured person** *for full explanation, see box below*

e.g. People who prefer literary novelists – such as Jonathan Franzen – sometimes look down on those who enjoy John Grisham, describing them as **groundlings**

'groundling' was originally a word referring to the lowliest kind of theatregoer during the reign of Queen Elizabeth I (1558–1603).

Such theatregoers could not afford a seat, but instead had to stand in the pit, which was known as the 'ground' at the time ('-ling', denoting a patronising diminutive, was then added to the end of the word).

This terribly snobbish term – after all, each 'groundling' had still bothered to show up to the theatre, and had paid good money to be there – persists today, to describe an uncultured person.

(my only) grouse (is) (set phrase) (verb) = **my only complaint is** a 'grouse' – meaning 'a complaint' in English – derives from the Old French, *groucier*: 'to grumble'; *note this grouse has nothing to do with the bird (the etymology of which, incidentally, is unknown)*

e.g. My only **grouse** about Danny Boyle's Olympics opening ceremony was that the Queen – whose interaction in the clip with James Bond was the highlight – didn't appear onscreen for longer

gulag

gulag (noun) = **a place so awful it calls to mind one of Stalin's forced labour camps** (pronounced '<u>goo</u>-lag') for full explanation, see box below

e.g. For today's mollycoddled youth, a house without wifi amounts to a **gulag**

'gulag' is a Russian term, used to refer to the hundreds of forced labour camps that existed in Soviet Russia between 1923 and 1961, roughly corresponding to Stalin's period in power (c. 1922–53). These awful camps were a major instrument of political repression, housing millions of Russians whom were deemed a threat to the state; half the inmates were imprisoned without trial (sometimes because of just one ill-timed joke). But the other reason for Stalin's supporting the 'gulags' was that – since the principle behind them was 'correction by forced labour' – the state benefited economically from the immensely cheap work undertaken by the prisoners.

*In the 'gulag' – the word is the Russian acronym for the Soviet agency in charge of the camps, '**G**(lavnoe) **u**(pravlenie ispravitel'no-trudovykh) **lag**(ereĭ)' (meaning, in English, 'Chief Administration for Corrective Labour Camps') – conditions were terrible, with meagre food rations, overcrowding and terrible hygiene: 1.6 million people (out of the 14 million who in total passed through the camps) died inside. And for those who got out alive, there was a lifelong ban on ever settling in big Russian cities, and on taking up certain kinds of employment (in fact, if you denied to a prospective boss that you'd been imprisoned in a camp – and this was found out – then you were imprisoned once more).*

The term was introduced to the West by Russian novelist Aleksandr Solzhenitsyn, via his book The Gulag Archipelago *(1973), which likened the disparate labour camps to a 'chain of islands' and described how the 'gulag', as a system, worked people to death. Today the term 'gulag' is used of any state-sponsored place of suffering, and has been applied liberally to Guantanamo Bay, the US dentention camp in Cuba, as well as to North Korea's prisons (with 'a gulag' being used either to refer to one such camp, or the collective noun 'the gulag' being employed for the entire system of interconnecting camps).*

---

gynarchy (noun) = **a society ruled by women** *(pronounced 'gahy-ner-kee')* from the Greek, *gyn-*: woman + *kratos*: power

e.g. Although we are now accustomed to female Presidents and Prime Ministers, there is still no example yet of a full-blown, 100 per cent male-free **gynarchy** in the West

hagridden by *(a negative emotion)* (set phrase) =
harassed by *(a negative emotion) for full explanation, see box below*

e.g. After his girlfriend left him, he was **hagridden** by self-doubt

---

*'hagridden' is a 17th-century word, a compound of 'hag': 'witch' +
'ridden': 'oppressed' (in the sense of 'ridden upon'). The original
meaning of 'hagridden' was 'afflicted by nightmares' and
specifically referred to the condition doctors now label 'sleep
paralysis'.*

*'Sleep paralysis' is the sensation that occurs to someone who's
just about to fall asleep and is in that transitional state between
wakefulness and slumber; it's characterised by complete muscle
weakness ('muscle atonia' is the medical term), meaning the
person afflicted is unable to move – despite being fully mentally
alert – and there is an accompanying feeling of a heavy weight
pinning the victim down against the bed; what's more, in the
background is the sense of a malevolent presence. This widely
recognised medical condition afflicts people at a time of worry in
their lives. 'Hagridden' is clearly an approximation of this feeling,
with the expression evoking the image of a 'hag' – an evil and
heavy force – 'riding' the victim, who is pinned to the bed as a
result.*

*Today, if we say someone is 'hagridden' by a negative emotion, we
mean they are very tormented by some mental anguish.*

---

hara-kiri (set phrase) = **elaborate suicide** *(pronounced 'hahr-uh-
keer-ee') for full explanation, see box below*

e.g. Once in a while, my laptop is prone to **hara-kiri**, necessitating
a visit to the computer shop

---

*'hara-kiri' is a Japanese word meaning 'belly cutting' , deriving
from 'hara': 'belly' + 'kiri': 'cutting' – and refers to a particularly
convoluted form of suicide. This involves the suicide victim firstly
cutting himself from left to right across the belly (causing
disembowelment), followed by a helpful assistant delivering a
killer blow and severing the victim's head from the body.*

Samurai – the military nobility in control of Japan until c. 1900 – would perform 'hara-kiri' in order to die with honour, rather than fall into the hands of their enemies. Before death, the fated man would be bathed, dressed in white robes and then have served to him his favourite meal; finally, he'd write a 'death poem' (a short poem where it was not done to refer to death directly, although metaphorical talk of 'setting suns' and 'falling leaves' was permitted). A crowd often watched, handily also acting as witness to the execution.

The practice all but died out at the end of the 19th century (as a result of the Samurai's own demise), although once in a while someone resurrects it in Japan. For example, in 2001, Japanese businessman Isao Inokuma, an ex-judo Olympics gold medal-winner whose business was in difficulty, performed hara-kiri. Today the term is generally used in a comical way, to refer to a suicide that makes a splash – usually of a metaphorical kind, such as a computer blowing up.

harridan (noun) = **a vicious old woman** *(pronounced 'hahr-i-den')* from the 16th-century French, *haridelle*: old horse; *in time, this meaning ungallantly evolved to encompass old women who were always angry*

e.g. Her critics attempted to depict Margaret Thatcher as a bullying **harridan**

harrier (noun) = **a persist attacker** *(pronounced 'har-ee-er')* from the Middle English, *hayrer*: a small hunting dog, associated with the *hare*, which this dog hunted

e.g. He experienced a surge of euphoria when he testified in court against his former boss and **harrier**

to haver (verb) = **to dither** *(pronounced 'hey-ver')* from the Scottish, *to haver*: to babble

e.g. She wasn't enjoying the Olympic shotput much, and soon found her hand **havering** over the remote control, ready to switch channels

hebdomadal (adj.) = **weekly** (*pronounced 'heb-<u>dom</u>-uh-dil'*) from the Greek, *hebdomas*: seven days' duration, from *hepta*: seven

e.g. The magazine *The Week* – as the name implies – is an **hebdomadal** publication

hecatomb (of) (noun) = **any great sacrifice (of)** (*pronounced '<u>hek</u>-a-toom'*) from the Greek, *hekatombe*: a hecatomb, from *hekaton*: hundred + *bous*: ox; *in ancient Greece, a 'hecatomb' was a sacrifice of exactly 100 oxen to the gods*

e.g. Almost one million British soldiers died in the **hecatomb of** World War I

to hector (someone) (verb) = **to bully (someone)** *for full explanation, see box below*

e.g. Harold Pinter's plays often feature one character **hectoring** another, with the playwright's signature sense of menace being the result

---

The verb 'to hector' comes from the Greek, 'Hektor', the greatest warrior for Troy in the Trojan War of Greek mythology.

Thus, in a nod to this noble warrior, the word 'to hector' was originally used in English of a hero; but then, when – in the mid-1600s – the term was applied to London street gangs, the sense irrevocably changed at this point, to mean 'to bully'.

---

hermetically sealed (set phrase) = *(of an environment)* **completely insulated from outside interference** (*'hermetically' is pronounced 'hur-<u>met</u>-ik-lee'*) *for full explanation, see box below*

e.g. Oxford dons live in colleges that are all but **hermetically sealed**, ensuring these great minds can pursue their studies in peace

---

The adjective 'hermetic' comes from the Latin form of the name of the god Hermes, which was 'hermeticus'.

Hermes was believed by the ancient Greeks to be able to magically seal a box in a certain way that ensured it could never be opened again, and this is the reason that the word 'hermetically' is used today to evoke a particularly airtight seal.

---

heterodox (adj.) = **unorthodox** *(pronounced 'het-er-uh-doks')* from the Greek, *heterodoxus*, from *heteros*: other + *doxa*: opinion

e.g. Any player who serves underarm in Wimbledon is embarking on a decidedly **heterodox** course

heuristic (noun) = **a rule of thumb (rather than a more scientific method)** *(pronounced 'yoo-ris-tik')* from the Greek, *heuriskein*: to find

e.g. To help aspiring writers, George Orwell invented a list of six **heuristics**, such as, 'If it is possible to cut a word out, always cut it out'

hijab (noun) = **a headscarf worn by Muslim women, covering the hair and neck** *(pronounced 'hih-jahb'); note that a 'burkha' – which is from a different Arabic word for 'veil' ('burqa') – covers both the entire body and the entire face, leaving just a mesh screen to see through* from the Arabic, *hijab*: a veil

e.g. A Muslim woman wearing a **hijab** and pushing a pram is a common sight on the high street

hireling (noun) = *(derogatory in tone)* **a person who works only for the money** from the English words, *hire* (giving the sense of 'a person for hire, for the best price') + *-ling* (the diminutive suffix)

e.g. Cynics say doctors advise patients to buy expensive drugs that they don't actually need and are really just **hirelings** of the big pharmaceutical companies

hoary old (set phrase) = *(of an idea)* **mouldy** *('hoary' is pronounced 'hawr-ee') for full explanation, see box below*

e.g. 'Time is a great healer' is the **hoary old** advice for anyone with a broken heart

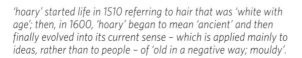

'hoary' started life in 1510 referring to hair that was 'white with age'; then, in 1600, 'hoary' began to mean 'ancient' and then finally evolved into its current sense – which is applied mainly to ideas, rather than to people – of 'old in a negative way; mouldy'.

Hobson's choice

Hobson's choice (set phrase) = **an apparently free choice, but one that offers no real alternative (and hence one that is not really a choice at all)** *for full explanation, see box below*

e.g. When asked by customers what colours his Ford Model T was available in, Henry Ford cited **Hobson's choice**, saying his car came in 'any colour you like, so long as it's black'

The phrase 'Hobson's choice' derives from Thomas Hobson (1554–1631), a stable-owner who ran a horse-rental business in Cambridge.

Hobson used to hire out horses – mainly to Cambridge University students – but refused to hire them out other than in the order he decided; more specifically, he was in the habit of giving his customers the 'choice' of the horse nearest the door or no horse at all.

Thirty years after Hobson's death, in 1660, the phrase 'Hobson's choice' was being used proverbially, and is still referenced today, in situations when there is no real choice at all.

---

hog-tied (by) (adj.) = **impeded (by)** *for full explanation, see box below*

e.g. Joan Collins has said of Cameron, 'I like David, but I think he's **hog-tied by** what's-his-name'

'hog-tied' comes from the English words 'hog' + 'tie', and originally referred to tying together the four legs of a pig (or 'hog') on a ranch, to keep the animal immobile whilst it was being branded.

A variation of this 'hog-tie' has been used to kill humans in a particularly gruesome way: firstly, the hands are tied together behind the victim's back; then the feet are bound together with a piece of rope which is also looped around the victim's neck. The tension on this neck rope can only be relieved if the neck and back are kept arched, but it's not possible for the victim to keep up this unnatural posture for long, and eventually he tires and strangles to death.

Today the term is thankfully mainly used metaphorically, to refer to a situation where someone's freedom is severely impinged upon.

hokey (adj.) = **corny** *(pronounced 'hoh-kee')* from the English word, *hokum*: a trite movie script

e.g. Critics of Disney films say the endings are predictable and **hokey**

Homeric (adj.) = *(of a situation)* **grand in size or style** *(pronounced 'hoh-mer-ik') for full explanation, see box below*

e.g. Some economists say that the creation of the euro currency – and all the problems resulting – is a tale of woe that is nothing short of **Homeric**

'Homeric' is used of a situation that is so grand in size or style that it might have made a fitting subject matter for a poem by the writer Homer (who lived c. 800 BC), the greatest epic poet of Ancient Greece.

Homer was the author of the two classic poems the Iliad *and the* Odyssey. *The* Iliad *is set during the Trojan War (the 10-year siege of the city of Troy by a group of Greek states) and encompasses many battles and events. Meanwhile, the* Odyssey *is a kind of sequel to it, and centres around the Greek hero Odysseus and his 10 years of wanderings after the fall of Troy. Odysseus encounters many perils during this time, such as the Sirens, who sang so enchantingly that they lured sailors to crash their ships on the rocky coast of the Sirens' island. But eventually Odysseus does get home and kills the suitors who had been harassing his wife during his absence.*

It's clear from this that Homer would only have been interested in writing about a subject that was meaty, with many twists and turns, and usually one that was tragic; so, when a situation is today described as 'Homeric', it means it's a tragedy of such epic proportions that Homer would be tempted to write about it.

homunculus (noun) = **a little man** *(pronounced 'huh-muhng-kyuh-luhs')* a diminutive of the Latin, *homo, hominis*: a man

e.g. For a leading man, Paul Newman – who was well under six feet tall – was something of a **homunculus**

to break the hoodoo (set phrase) = **to break a run of bad luck**
from the American English word 'hoodoo': 'someone who practices
voodoo (black magic)', in 1870; the sense evolved in 1880 to mean
'something causing bad luck'

e.g. The football team hadn't won a title for 10 years, but the
hiring of a new coach soon **broke the hoodoo**

hyperreal (adj.) = *(of a piece of art)* **extremely realistic in detail**
from the English words *hyper + real*

e.g. Many critics have praised the film *Drive*, a **hyperreal**
adaptation of a novel by American writer James Sallis that is
centred around driving and violence and is particularly gritty

Iago-like = *(of a person)* **very treacherous**
('Iago' is pronounced 'eye-ar-go') for full
explanation, see box below

e.g. After the Italian media alleged that the
Pope's butler was behind the leaking of
confidential Vatican papers, many were
quick to label the butler an **Iago-like** traitor

*'Iago' is the name of the treacherous villain in Shakespeare's
tragedy* Othello *(1601–4). A soldier who fought beside Othello (a
Moorish general) for many years, Iago is Othello's trusted junior
and adviser.*

*But Iago, in fact, hates Othello – although no official motive is
provided by Shakespeare, jealousy of Othello's elevated social
status is suspected as the reason – and so devises a plan to
destroy him, by making Othello believe that his wife is having an
affair with a lieutenant. In the end, Othello, believing Iago's lies
about his wife, kills her; but Iago's treachery is then finally
revealed – by his own wife.*

*Today we reserve the term 'Iago-like' for the kind of person who is
in a position of trust but who then betrays this in spectacular
fashion.*

(the) id; ego; and superego

(the) id; ego; and superego (noun) = *(of humans)* subconscious passions; conscious thought; and the conscience itself *for full explanation, see box below*

e.g. The **id** drives someone on a diet to reach for that extra cookie; 'OK, but just this once' says the ego; but then the **superego** wades in and prevails, citing the longer-lasting glow of self-restraint and urging abstinence

---

Tired of hearing the woolly phrase 'the unconscious', Sigmund Freud (1856–1939) invented these three terms – the 'id'; 'ego'; and 'superego' – so he could be more precise when describing the mental lives of humans.

In his work The Ego and the Id *(1923), Freud explained that the 'id' seeks instant self-gratification, and is not conscious – so the 'id' can be thought of as 'animal instinct' (reflected in the Latin meaning of 'id', which is 'it'). The 'ego' (which means the more human 'I' in Latin), though, is a kind of safety mechanism, sometimes overruling the 'id' and stopping the 'id' from having its way, especially if physical harm would result. However, most of the time, the 'ego' is soft on the 'id', and produces some mental gymnastics (such as rationalisation or denial) in order to indulge the base instinct of the 'id'. Freud used the analogy of the 'id' as a wild horse, and the 'ego' as the man on the horse's back, attempting to control it, before giving in. (Note that Freud's definition of 'ego' has nothing to do with the defintion of 'ego' prevalent today, such as in the phrase 'he has a big ego'.)*

And finally, the 'superego' (which is 'above the ego' and so, almost God-like) is our conscience, explaining to us the moral – rather than the physical – consequences if we actually go ahead and follow the urges of the 'id' (which has at this stage convinced the 'ego' of the merits of its scheme).

---

immiseration (noun) = **impoverishment** *(pronounced 'ih-mis-uh-rey-shun')* from the English words, *in-* + *miserable* + *-ation*

e.g. The novels of Charles Dickens concern people – such as Oliver Twist – who try to rise above their lives of **immiseration**

self-immolation (noun) = **the deliberate sacrifice of oneself, by setting oneself alight** *('immolation' is pronounced 'im-uh-ley-shuhn')* from the Latin, *immolatio*: a sacrifice

e.g. The Arab Spring was started by the **self-immolation** of a fruit vendor in Tunisia who – as a protest against police corruption – set himself alight

to immure (verb) = **to shut someone in, against their will** *(pronounced 'ih-myoor')* from the Latin, *immurare*: to enclose, from *in-*: in + *murus*: wall

e.g. It was soon after he was spotted scratching the ground and making clucking sounds that my uncle was **immured** in a lunatic asylum

impassable (adj.) = **insurmountable** *(pronounced 'im-pas-uh-buhl')* from the English words, *im-* (expressing a negative) + *passable*; *'impassable' literally means 'cannot be passed'*

e.g. If an **impassable** division develops between a couple, they will often divorce

impedimenta (plural noun) = **bulky equipment for an activity** *(pronounced 'im-ped-uh-men-tuh')* from the Latin plural of *impedimentum*: impediment, from *impedire*: to impede

e.g. On the day that the very last Harry Potter book was published, there appeared on the street outside bookshops up and down the country a huge queue of fans sporting Hogwarts **impedimenta**

impolitic (adj.) = **unwise** *(pronounced 'im-pol-i-tik')* from the English words, *in-* + *politic*, from the French, *politique*, from the Latin, *politicus*: civil

e.g. If someone else is treating you to dinner, it's **impolitic** to order the most expensive bottle of wine on the menu

to importune (someone to something) (verb) = **to ask (someone) persistently to do something** *(pronounced 'im-pawr-toon')* from the Latin, *importunus*: troublesome; *originally the Latin 'importunus' had a more literal meaning, describing a place 'having no harbour' (i.e. 'troublesome for a ship to access'), from 'in-': not + 'portus': harbour*

e.g. After she said 'no' to his marriage proposal, he **importuned** her every day to accept his invitation, until she eventually cracked

to mutter imprecations (set phrase) = **to mutter curses** *('imprecations' are pronounced 'im-pri-key-shuhns')* from the Latin, *imprecari*: to curse, from *in-*: toward + *precari*: to pray

e.g. The Olympic athlete came last in the race, then rolled around in the dust, muttering **imprecations**

imprest funds (set phrase) = **funds for paying small expenditures, topped up periodically** *('imprest' is pronounced 'im-prest')* from the obsolete Italian, *imprestare*: to lend, from the Latin, *in-*: toward + *prestare*: to lend

e.g. He saw the coffee tin was empty, so headed in the direction of the secretary's desk, where the **imprest funds** were kept in a jar

to impugn (someone or something) (verb) = **to verbally attack (someone or something)** *(pronounced 'im-pyoon')* from the Latin, *impugnare*: to assail, from *in-*: toward + *pugnare*: to fight

e.g. In the run-up to the US Presidential elections, the two main opponents spend much of their time **impugning** each other's character on TV

to impute (something) to (something) = **to ascribe (something) to (something)** from the Latin, *imputare*: to ascribe, from *in-*: toward + *putare*: to think

e.g. The airline **imputed** the plane crash **to** a faulty engine

inalienable rights (set phrase) = **rights that cannot be taken away** *(pronounced 'in-ey-lee-uh-nuh-buhl')* from the English words, *in-*: not (from the Latin, *in*: not) + *alienable*: capable of being transferred to another; from the Latin, *alienare*: to make another's (and, hence, to estrange); from *alius*: another; *'inalienable rights' literally means 'rights that cannot be transferred to another'*

e.g. People feel safe buying property in the United Kingdom since the country has laws setting out citizens' **inalienable rights**

inamorata (noun) = **a woman with whom one is in love**
(pronounced 'in-am-uh-rah-tuh') from the Italian, *inamorata*: the
enamoured one, past participle of the verb *inamorare*, based on the
Latin, *amor*: love

e.g. When Obama took Michelle out for a date night in New York
– including a dinner at Bluehill Restaurant (renowned for its
'locally grown fare'), and a Broadway show – photographers
swarmed around the President and his **inamorata**

incantation (noun) = **a conventional utterance, repeated
without thinking** from the Latin, *incantare*: to chant

e.g. The Queen must be used to people firing sycophantic
incantations in her direction

indefatigable (adj.) = **tireless** *(pronounced 'in-di-fat-i-guh-buhl')*
from the Latin, *indefatigabilis*: that cannot be tired out, from *in-*: not
+ *defatigare*: to tire out

e.g. The actor Richard Burton was such an **indefatigable**
fornicator that – according to one commentator – 'he made Errol
Flynn look like the head of the Cistercian order of monks'

to induce from (a specific situation) that (verb) = **to
work out a general rule from (a specific situation) that** from the
Latin, *inducere*: to lead in, from *in-*: into + *ducere*: to lead

e.g. She refused to tell him where she'd spent the night, and he
induced from her silence **that** she was having an affair

infra dig (set phrase) = **beneath one's dignity,
demeaning** from the Latin, *infra dignitatem*:
beneath one's dignity

e.g. Some snobs used to consider rosé wine to
be **infra dig**, but now it's considered very
acceptable

inkhorn terms (set phrase) = **pedantic terms** from the
14th-century English word, *inkhorn*: a small container –
originally made out of an animal's horn – for holding ink,
beloved of scribblers (as are 'inkhorn terms')

e.g. In his interviews, the painter David Hockney is
refreshingly free of the **inkhorn terms** common to the art
critics who comment on his work

to inter (someone)

to inter (someone) (verb) = **to bury (someone)** *(pronounced 'in-tur')* from the Latin, *in-*: into + *terra*: earth

e.g. When he started insisting on eating cat food for breakfast, his family took the decision to **inter** him in a lunatic asylum

intractable (adj.) = **uncontrollable;** *note that the opposite,* **'tractable', means 'controllable'** *(pronounced 'in-trak-tuh-buhl')* from the Latin, *intractabilis*, from *in-*: not + *tractare:* to handle

e.g. Police officers are rumoured to use rubber battons to beat **intractable** prisoners

insensate (adj.) = **lacking sensation** *(pronounced 'in-sen-seyt')* from the Latin, *insensatus*, from *in-*: not + *sensatus*: having senses

e.g. For years, coma victims can lie in hospital beds in a totally **insensate** state

to interdict (verb) = **to forbid (something)** from the Latin, *interdicere*: to forbid by decree, from *inter-*: between and *dicere*: to say

e.g. In the United States, for people under 21 years old, alcohol is **interdicted**

interlocutor (noun) = **a person who participates in a conversation** *(pronounced 'in-ter-lok-yuh-ter')* from the Latin, *interlocut-*: interrupted (by speech), from *interloqui*, from *inter-*: between + *loqui*: to speak

e.g. The English often communicate not by saying what's on their mind, but by hoping their **interlocutor** will correctly interpret a twitch of the forehead or a mournful wipe of the nose

interloper (noun) = **an intruder** from *inter-*: amidst + *loper*: to leap, from the Middle Dutch, *loopen*: to leap

e.g. Federer has dominated men's tennis for so long that, when anyone else wins Wimbledon, they almost look like an **interloper**

interpolation (noun) = **a remark inserted into a conversation** *(pronounced 'in-tur-puh-ley-shuhn')* from the Latin, *interpolare*: to alter, from *inter-*: between + *polare*, related to *polire*: to polish

e.g. Adults bemoan teenagers who can't complete a sentence without the mandatory **interpolation** of the words 'like' or 'kind of'

interstices (pl. noun) = **spaces between objects** (*pronounced 'in-tur-stis-ees'*) from the Latin, *intersistere*: to stand between, from *inter*: between + *sistere*: to stand

e.g. People who read memoirs accept that some fiction often creeps into the **interstices** between facts

intransigent (adj.) = **uncompromising** (*pronounced 'in-tran-si-juhnt'*) from the Latin, *in-*: not + *transigere*: to come to an agreement

e.g. Critics of Steve Jobs say he was an **intransigent** ego maniac

ipso facto (set phrase) = **by the very fact itself** from the Latin, *ipso facto*: by that very fact

e.g. The enemy of one's enemy is **ipso facto** one's friend

iridescent (adj.) = **displaying rainbow-like colours** (*pronounced 'ir-i-des-uhnt'*) from the Latin, *iris, irid-*: rainbow + *-escent*

e.g. My wife enjoys relaxing in the bath with a gin and tonic, surrounded by **iridescent** bubbles that pop periodically

irredentist (noun, or adj.) = **a person advocating the return to their country of any territory historically belonging to it, but currently occupied by foreigners** (*pronounced 'ir-i-den-tist'*) from the Italian, (*Italia*) *irredenta*: unredeemed (Italy); *the word 'irrendentist' derives from 19th-century politics, to describe an Italian politican who advocated the return to Italy of all neighbouring Italian-speaking regions (such as Corsica)*

e.g. Britain is continually urging Argentina to abandon their **irredentist** policy towards the Falklands, and allow the islanders to decide their own allegiance

irrefragable (adj.) = **(of a fact) not to be contested** (*pronounced 'ih-ref-ruh-guh-buhl'*) from the Latin, *irrefragabilis*, from *in-*: not + *refragari*: to contest, from *re-*: back + *frag-*, based on *frangere*: to break

e.g. It's an **irrefragable** fact that – after he died in the car crash in Paris that also killed Princess Diana – the chauffeur Henri Paul had a blood alcohol content level more than three times the threshold for drink driving under French law

isomorphic (adj.) = **having the same appearance** from the Greek, *isos*: same + *morphe*: shape

e.g. Some say that Britney Spears and Taylor Swift – all blonde hair and tight jeans – are **isomorphic**

iteration (noun) = **a repeated performance** from the Latin, *iterare*: to repeat, from *iterum*: again

e.g. As the Presidential election approached, Americans prepared themselves for yet another **iteration** of mud-slinging and promises of change

J

Jamesian (adj.) = *(of a novel)* **psychologically insightful** *(as Henry James's novels were)* *(pronounced 'jeym-zee-uhn')* for full explanation, see box below

e.g. The novelist Alan Hollinghurst has been praised by critic Adam Kirsch for a 'truly **Jamesian** fineness of perception, his own consciousness darting around those of his characters, recording every desire and hesitation and misunderstanding'

Henry James (1843–1916) was an American writer, most famous for his novels depicting Americans encountering Europe and the Europeans. He employed techniques such as interior monologues (for characters) and unreliable narrators to imbue his fiction with a more realistic atmosphere than his peers.

So deft was his approach that it has been compared to impressionist painting, in the way he explored issues of consciousness and perception within his characters. Some critics have gone so far as to describe James's novels as psychological thought experiments.

For example, his most famous work The Portrait of a Lady *(1881) might be seen as a study in what happens to a young lady who suddenly becomes very rich. Set in England and Italy, this novel concerns a spirited young American woman who inherits a large amount of money and then falls victim to scheming by two American expatriates. The novel is deeply psychological (exploring the minds of its characters in great depth, and also the difference between the old world of Europe and the new world of America), and when we use the word 'Jamesian' today to describe a book, we imply a similarly high degree of psychological probing.*

---

jeu d'esprit (noun) = **a light-hearted display of wit** *(pronounced 'juh-des-pree')* from the French, *jeu d'esprit*: play of the mind

e.g. A love affair enjoyed by Shakespeare at the time he was writing *Romeo and Juliet* is the subject of Tom Stoppard's **jeu d'esprit** *Shakespeare in Love* (1998)

jeunesse dorée

jeunesse dorée (set phrase) = **stylish, wealthy young people**
(pronounced 'juh-nes daw-rey') for full explanation, see box below

e.g. Since they have no need for remunerative (but tedious) jobs in banking or law, New York's **jeunesse dorée** often instead pursue creative-writing courses

---

'jeunesse dorée' means 'gilded youth' in French, and is the name given by the French to a group of young dandies who, after the execution of Robespierre – the leader of the French Revolution (1789–99) – fought to reinstall the old order and the artistocracy, using wooden clubs to attack the poor who supported the Revolution.

Sartorially elegant, the 'jeunesse dorée' wore tight coats with large, colourful lapels and elaborately knotted cravats. They had their own subculture, including affectations of speech and designated meeting places in certain chic cafés.

Today the phrase 'jeunesse dorée' is used to refer to the similarly fashionable – and often spoilt – offspring of the wealthy.

---

to keen (verb) = *(of mourners)* **to wail** from the Irish, *caoinim*: I wail

e.g. JFK was perturbed by his phone call with Marilyn Monroe, for her voice had a **keening** quality to it

kinetic (adj.) = *(of an artwork)* **involving motion for its effect** from the Greek, *kinetikos*, from *kinein*: to move

e.g. A child's mobile – placed over a cot – is an example of **kinetic** art: for the mobile's ability to enthrall depends on its moving with the slightest air current

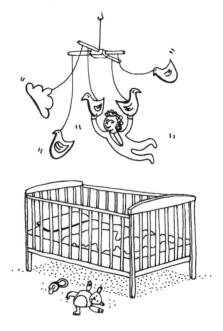

kouros (noun) = **a Greek statue of a naked youth** *(pronounced 'koor-os')* from the Greek, *koros*: boy

e.g. On the lawns of some English country houses, a delapidated **kouros** stands alone

to kowtow to (someone) (verb) = **to act submissively towards (someone)** *(pronounced 'cow-tauw')* from the Chinese, *ketou, from ke*: knock + *tou*: head; *'to kowtow' literally means 'to kneel and touch the ground with the forehead in submission, as per an ancient Chinese custom'*

e.g. The good thing about being self-employed is you don't have to **kowtow to** a boss

to kvetch about (something) (verb) = **to complain about (something)** *(pronounced 'kvech')* from the Yiddish, *kvetshn*: to complain, ultimately from the Middle High German, *quetschen*: to complain

e.g. Older people often **kvetch about** the behaviour of today's youth

L

labile (set phrase) = **unstable** (*pronounced 'lay-bile'*) from the Latin, *labilis*: apt to slip, from *labi*: to slip

e.g. The date went badly: after she laughed uncontrollably for a full five minutes when he asked her, 'How are you?', he realised he was dealing with an emotionally **labile** individual

lantern-jawed (adj.) = **with a jutting lower jaw**
the phrase 'lantern-jawed' came about because such a jaw gives its owner such a gaunt face, apparently resembling a lantern

e.g. If you're **lantern-jawed**, you're unlikely to make it as a Hollywood leading man

latitudinarian (adj.) = *(of a person)* **broad-minded** (*pronounced 'lat-i-tuden-air-ee-uhn'*) from the Latin, *latitudo*: breadth

e.g. Christianity is split between **latitudinarian** thinkers (who seek to fit religious teaching to modern trends) and orthodox Christians (who try to uphold traditional religious concepts)

latrine (noun) = **a toilet in a public place, like a hospital** (*pronounced 'luh-treen'*) from the Latin, *latrina*, a contraction of *lavatrina*: a washroom, from *lavare*: to wash

e.g. The patient suffering from gastroenteritis had left the **latrine** in a pitiful condition

Lebensraum

Lebensraum (noun) = *(of an area of land)* territory sought for occupation by a nation whose own population is expanding *(pronounced 'ley-buhns-raum')* for full explanation, see box below

e.g. With their pushes into Tibet and other territories, critics have accused China of pursuing a modern-day policy of **Lebensraum**

'Lebensraum' is a German word meaning 'living space', deriving from the German words for 'life' ('Leben') and for 'space' ('Raum'). The term 'Lebensraum' – which was invented in Germany in 1901 – is most associated with the Nazis.

In his book Mein Kampf *(1925) – which translates as* My Struggle *– Hitler detailed his belief that the growing German population should look to Eastern Europe for 'Lebensraum' (i.e. land and raw materials). Later, the Führer used 'Lebensraum' as a key justification for the expansionist policies of Nazi Germany.*

To secure these territories, the Nazis – who believed themselves a superior race – planned to either deport or exterminate the urban population of Eastern Europe by starvation, thus creating an agricultural surplus for the Germanic people, who would come in and occupy the empty land. (To Nazi minds, this whole policy had the added benefit of killing off inferior races.) In 1939, Germany invaded Poland and enacted this plan. Today, this highly charged term is still used, if one nation is seeking to displace another from its dwelling place.

(the) lee (of) (noun) = **the side (of a building) protected from the wind** from the Old English, *hleo*: shelter, related to the Old Norse, *hle*: shelter

e.g. Since it was windy, he decided to set up his barbeque in **the lee of** the house

leitmotif (noun) = *(within art)* **a recurring theme** *(pronounced 'light-moh-teef')* from the German, *Leitmotiv*: leading motif, from *leit*-: leading (from *leiten*: to lead) + *Motiv*: motif

e.g. Throughout Hitchcock's horror films, death by strangulation is a **leitmotif**

the Levant (noun) = *(collective noun)* **the countries bordering the Eastern Mediterranean Sea (i.e. Iraq, Israel, Palestine, Syria, Lebanon, Jordan, Cyprus, Turkey)** *(pronounced 'Lev-ant') for full explanation, see box below*

e.g. The first course – which consisted of hummus, falafel and tabbouleh – had more than a touch of the **Levant** about it

---

'the Levant' is from the French, 'levant': 'rising' (present participle of 'lever': 'to lift, rise') – in other words, 'the Levant' means 'the point where the sun lifts, or rises' (i.e.'the East').

(And note that, obversely, 'the Occident' – which means 'the West' – derives from the Latin present participle of 'occidere': 'to fall down'; in other words, 'the point where the sun falls down, or sets', i.e. 'the West'.)

'The Levant' is today a collective phrase, to sum up both geographically and culturally, those countries – listed above – bordering the Eastern Mediterranean Sea.

---

libation (noun) = *(facetious in tone)* **an alcoholic drink** *(pronounced 'lie-bey-shuhn') for full explanation, see box below*

e.g. After his daughter was born, he celebrated with champagne, his preferred **libation**

'libation' derives from the the Latin, 'libare': 'to pour out as an offering to the gods'. In Ancient Greece, a 'libation' was a ritual pouring out of a liquid – usually a mixture of wine and water in a jug, poured from a height into a shallow bowl – as an offering to a god. This happened at the start of meals.

Today the practice is still seen, but usually as a way of remembering those who have died (rather than as a way of honouring the gods). In Russia, for example, it's still an old tradition to pour out vodka onto someone's grave; and, to commemorate dead friends, African-American rappers sometimes pour out a libation from a whisky bottle, before drinking the whisky themselves: a practice referred to as 'tipping to one's (dead) homies' or 'pouring one out'.

The word 'libation' generally, though, carries a facetious sense nowadays, and simply refers to any alcoholic drink in a mock pompous – and therefore humorous – way.

105

libretto (noun) = **the text of an opera** (pronounced 'li-<u>bret</u>-oh') from the Italian, *libretto*, the diminutive of *libro*: book, from the Latin, *liber*: book

e.g. Ian McEwan, author of the novel *Atonement*, also writes **librettos**, such as that for the opera *For You*, which is about an ageing composer

like so much (+ singular noun) / like so many (+ plural noun) (set phrase) = *(of the plural noun)* **like an exactly equivalent amount of (+ noun)** *note that the phrases 'like so much' (+ singular noun) and 'like so many' (+ plural noun) precede a poetic image*

e.g. He challenged him to a duel, then sliced him up **like so much** beef

and

e.g. The onlookers turned on the speaker **like so many** tigers

lily-livered (adj.) = **cowardly** *for full explanation, see box below*

e.g. Politicians are forever trying to depict themselves as bold and their opponents as **lily-livered**

In medieval times, the liver was believed to be where courage resided in a person. So, to medieval minds, someone courageous must have had a red (i.e. healthy) liver; but a coward was supposed to possess a white, 'lily-coloured' (i.e. unhealthy) liver, devoid of blood.

The most famous incidence of the term is in Macbeth *(1605), although it's not known if Shakespeare himself invented the phrase. Today 'lily-livered' is still often used as a poetic way of calling someone a coward.*

---

to limn (something) (verb) = **to depict** (pronounced 'lim') from the Old French, *luminer*: to illuminate, from the Latin, *luminare*: to make light

e.g. Graham Greene's collection of letters **limn** a troubled, but insightful, personality

lineament (noun) = **distinctive feature** (*pronounced 'lin-ee-uh-muhnt'*) from the Latin, *lineamentum*, from *lineare*: to make straight, from *linea*: a line

e.g. After the cat bit his hand, pain was depicted in every **lineament** of his face

littoral (adj.) = **of a shore** (*pronounced 'literal'*) from the Latin, *litus, littoris*: a shore

e.g. He used his retirement money to buy a **littoral** property, then spent his twilight years watching the ocean from his living room

locus (noun) = **a place that is a centre of activity** (*pronounced 'low-kuhs'*) from the Latin, *locus*: place

e.g. The **locus** of the UK government is number 10 Downing Street

longueurs (pl. noun) = *(of a novel or play)* **a tedious patch** (*pronounced 'long-ur'*) from the French, *longueur*: length

e.g. Many of the audience members fell asleep because the play was riddled with **longueurs**

louring sky (set phrase) = **threatening sky** (*pronounced 'lou-uhr-ing'*) the word '*louring*' is a variant spelling of '*lowering*'

e.g. To convey the impression of doom, the *Lord of the Rings* trilogy features many a **louring sky**

lubricious (adj.) = **lewd** (*pronounced 'loo-brish-uhs'*) from the Latin, *lubricus*: slippery; in English, '*lubricious*' literally means '*having a slippery quaility*'

e.g. The novel *Fifty Shades of Grey* describes various acts in **lubricious** detail

lucubrations (pl. noun) = **pretentious writing** (*pronounced 'luck-yoo-brey-shuhns'*) from the Latin, *lucubratio*, from *lucubrare*: to work at night by lamplight (*i.e. to have worked too many hours on a piece of writing, leading to too-careful elaboration, and, so, to the pretentious kind of writing that the word 'lucubrations' implies*)

e.g. The public views academics as being lost in their own **lucubrations**

Lucullan

Lucullan (adj.) = *(of food)* **lavish** *(pronounced 'luck-kuhl-uhn') for full explanation, see box below*

e.g. Kim Jong Il of North Korea had fresh fish flown in from Japan: he liked to eat the resulting sashimi so fresh that he insisted the mouth of the fish still be moving when he took his first bite (to keep the fish twitching, Kim's chef avoided the vital organs): such **Lucullan** meals were typical of the North Korean leader

---

'Lucullan' derives from the name of Licinius Lucullus, a Roman general from the 1st century BC famous for the fine banquets he laid on for guests.

So obsessed was Lucullus with food that, when, one night, his servants served him only one paltry course for dinner – simply because Lucullus was dining alone that particular evening – Lucullus asked them where the rest of the food was, demanding in a fit of gluttonous egomania, 'What, did not you know, then, that today Lucullus dines with Lucullus?'

Lucullus introduced the cherry and the apricot to Rome, and was the only person in the city who could provide thrushes for gastronomic purposes all year round – he had his own breeding pens for the very purpose. It's not much of a surprise, then, that today we use 'Lucullan' to describe a 'very lavish' banquet.

---

lumpen (adj.) = *(of a person)* **vulgar and mentally slow** *for full explanation, see box below*

e.g. By plunging ourselves into Nigella Lawson's extravagantly coloured cookbooks, we escape our own **lumpen** existences

---

'lumpen' is a shortened form of the German word, 'lumpenproletariat', a term coined by Karl Marx (1818–83) to describe those people – mainly the criminally-minded and the unemployed – who were (according to Marx) totally uninterested in revolutionary advancement.

'lumpenproletariat' derives from the German words 'lumpen': 'a ragamuffin' and 'proletariat': 'proletarian', which originated from the Latin 'proles': 'offspring' (because the Romans used the term 'proles' to denote a person who had no wealth in property, and who consequently paid no taxes and therefore only really served the state by producing offspring).

It was in his book The German Ideology *(1845) that Marx defined the 'lumpenproletariat' as being that layer of the working class unlikely to ever achieve class consciousness, or to produce anything socially useful, and therefore unhelpful to revolutionary advancement. In another book, Marx is more specific about this 'refuse of all classes', listing its members as 'swindlers, confidence tricksters, brothel-keepers, rag-and-bone merchants, beggars, and other flotsam of society'. Today 'lumpen' describes a vulgar person, with the extra connotation of the mental sluggishness Marx identified in this underclass.*

to mainline (a drug) (verb) = *(informal in tone)* **to introduce (a drug) directly into the body** from the English words invented in 1841, *main line*: literally 'the principal line of a railway'; *from 1933, a 'main line' began to mean, in American-English slang, 'the main vein into which drugs can be injected'*

e.g. On stag weekends, young men sit around in pubs in Central Europe, **mainlining** beer like it is oxygen

major domo (noun) = **one who makes arrangements for another** *(pronounced 'mey-jer-doh-mow')* from the Latin, *major domo*: chief of the household, from the Latin, *major*: greater + *domo*: of the household (the genitive of *domus*: household)

e.g. The White House **major domo** frowned as another nubile young lady was ushered into JFK's personal quarters

makeweight (noun) = **an unimportant person or thing, added so as to make up a lack** from the English words, *make + weight; a makeweight literally refers to 'an object put on a scale to make up the required weight'*

e.g. The first part of President Nixon's speech was well received; but the second part consisted of **makeweight** arguments

Malthusian catastrophe (set phrase) = **the problems resulting from overpopulation** *('Malthusian' is pronounced 'mal-thoo-zhi-uhn') for full explanation, see box below*

e.g. Critics blame the Catholic church – and its ban on artificial contraception – for an unfolding **Malthusian catastrophe**

The phrase derives from Thomas Robert Malthus, an English clergyman, who, in Essay on Population *(1798), argued that, unless 'moral restraint' (i.e. sexual abstinence) was practised, the world's population would increase at a greater rate than its means of subsistence, resulting in catastrophes such as war, famine and other unpleasantries.*

Man has, though, avoided a Malthusian nightmare over the past two centuries, and Malthus's dire predictions have been proven wrong. The reason? Malthus failed to foresee man's ingenuity in developing new technologies to better exploit the planet's resources – so food production, for example, has in fact kept pace with population growth, rather than failing to match it (which would have led to mass starvation, as Malthus incorrectly prognosticated).

But, regardless of the inaccuracy of his predictions, Malthus's name is still evoked today, when we speak of overpopulation fears and our concerns this will lead to a 'Malthusian catastrophe'.

---

mantle (noun) = **a covering** from the Latin, *mantellum*: cloak; *a 'mantle' literally refers to a loose, sleeveless coat worn over outer garments*

e.g. In order to keep society functioning smoothly, everyone has implicitly agreed to curb their animal instincts, and to instead don a **mantle** of decorum

marquee name (set phrase) = **a big name** *(within an industry like showbusiness)* for full *explanation, see box below*

e.g. It took many years of eeking out a living by writing pieces such as *The History of Pea Eating* – a satirical discussion about the various attempts mankind has made over the centuries to successfully eat peas – before Alfred Hitchcock turned his skills to the movies and became a **marquee name**

'marquee' as an adjective – as used in 'marquee name' – derived from 'marquee' as a noun (meaning 'a rooflike projection over the entrance to a building', first recorded in 1912).

A 'marquee name' would therefore be the name of an entertainer who was sufficiently famous to act as a draw for crowds, once his name was placed on the 'marquee' over the entrance to a theatre.

(style) maven (set phrase) = **a (style) expert** *('maven' is pronounced 'mey-vuhn')* from the Yiddish, *myven,* from the Hebrew, *mebhin*: one who understands

e.g. **Style maven** Coco Chanel started using morphine aggressively in her fifties, injecting herself on a daily basis until her death aged 87

melisma (noun) = **a group of many notes sung to just one syllable of text, producing a kind of warble** *(pronounced 'mi-liz-muh')* from the Greek, *melisma*: melody

e.g. Karaoke nights are characterised by drunken people belting out **melisma**-heavy songs

memento mori (set phrase) = **an object that serves as a reminder of death, like a skull** *('mori' is pronounced 'mor-ee')* from the Latin, *memento mori*: remember (that you have) to die

e.g. Damien Hirst's sculpture *For the Love of God* consists of a platinum skull encrusted with 8,601 flawless diamonds: a shimmering **memento mori** that allegedly sold for £50m

mendicant (adj.) = **prone to begging** *(pronounced 'men-di-kuhnt')* from the Latin, *mendicare*: to beg

e.g. Critics say that Scotland is a **mendicant** nation, always looking for more contributions from its larger neighbour

meniscus (noun) = **a tiny barrier; *literally referring to the thin cartilage between the articulating ends of the bones in a joint such as the knee*** *(pronounced 'mi-nis-kuhs')* from the Greek, *meniskos*: crescent

e.g. The coming of age novel *The Catcher in the Rye* pokes at the **meniscus** that separates the innocence of childhood from the knowingness of adulthood

Mephistophelean (adj.) = **very evil**
(pronounced 'mef-uh-stof-alien') for full explanation, see box below

e.g. Africa has had more than its fair share of **Mephistophelean** dictators, who have presided over child armies and the rumoured cannibalism of their enemies

Mephistopheles is the envoy of the Devil in the Faust legend, which started in Germany in the 16th century.

Faust was a highly successful scholar, but also dissatisfied with his life, and so made a deal with the Devil, exchanging his soul for unlimited knowledge and worldly pleasures (and giving birth to the phrase, 'making a deal with the Devil').

In response, the Devil's representative, Mephistopheles, appears. The Devil makes a bargain with Faust: Mephistopheles will put his magical powers at Faust's disposal for a fixed term of 24 years but, once this time has lapsed, the Devil will claim Faust's soul and Faust will be eternally damned. Amongst other dastardly deeds, Mephistopheles helps Faust seduce a beautiful and innocent girl, Gretchen, whose life is ultimately destroyed. In the end, Faust is left irrevocably corrupted and, when the 24 years of high living are over, the Devil does indeed carry him off to hell. 'Mephistophelean' is still used today, to describe a person of great evil.

mercantilist (adj.) = **believing in the benefits to a nation that accrue from profitable trading with other nations** (*pronounced 'mur-kuhn-ti-lizt') for full explanation, see box below*

e.g. Critics say that Germany's initial reluctance to bail out its eurozone neighbours is because Germany – whose exports have boomed since the creation of the euro – wants to continue subjecting other European nations to **mercantilist** exploitation

'mercantilist' derives from 'mercantilism', a theory prevalent in Europe during the 17th and 18th centuries, stating that the wealth of a nation depends on how big its pool of precious metals is.

According to the theory, the government of every nation should aim to export more than it imports (using the proceeds to accumulate precious metals), and also, to further national commercial interests by such activities as establishing colonies.

mesomorph

mesomorph (noun) = **a person with a compact, muscular build** (*pronounced 'mez-uh-mawrf') for full explanation, see box below*

e.g. Airport magazines are littered with stories of female celebrities who have given up weight training and the accompanying **mesomorph**-shaped body, in favour of just eating sensibly

---

'mesomorph' derives from the Greek, 'mesos': 'middle' + 'morphe': 'form'.

More specifically, 'mesos' is a reference to the mesodermal layer of the embryo: the middle germ layer of an animal embryo, which ultimately gives rise to muscle (explaining why it is that a muscular body shape is labelled 'mesomorph').

---

messianic (adj.) = **fervent** (*pronounced 'messy-arnik'*) from the French, *messianique*: messianic, itself from *Messie*: Messiah, and both ultimately from the Hebrew, *masiah*: anointed; *the word 'Messianic' literally refers to Jesus, regarded by Christians as the Messiah of the Hebrew prophecies*

e.g. In his later years, Charles M. Schulz, creator of *Peanuts*, experienced hand tremors – as a result of Parkinson's Disease – that were so severe he had to hold onto the side of his desk with one hand to keep himself steady; but such was his **messianic** zeal to produce a cartoon strip each and every day, that this didn't impede his ouput

mimsy (adj.) = ineffectual *for full explanation, see box below*

e.g. Oxford University as depicted in *Brideshead Revisited* is populated exclusively by **mimsy** public school boys, clutching teddy bears to their chests

'*mimsy*' *is a word invented by Lewis Carroll, which appears in his poem 'Jabberwocky', a work stumbled across by Alice in Carroll's novel* Through the Looking-Glass, and What Alice Found There *(1872), the sequel to the more famous Alice's Adventures in Wonderland.*

The poem 'Jabberwocky' – which tells of a strange creature, the Jabberwock – is a work of nonsense, read aloud by the very confused Alice, who is already befuddled, having stepped into the back-to-front world of the looking glass.

The third line of the poem reads, 'All mimsy were the borogroves'. In a book note later, Carroll describes a 'borogrove' as 'an extinct kind of parrot. They had no wings, beaks turned up, made their nests under sun-dials and lived on veal'; and the poet also tells us the meaning of 'mimsy', which, it turns out, is a combination of two words: 'flimsy' and 'miserable'. (Incidentally, most critics agree that Carroll wrote the poem to satirise other pretentious poems which, despite using more conventional words, are still impossible to understand.)

minatory (adj.) = *(formal in tone)* **threatening** (pronounced '*min-uh-tohr-ee*') from the Latin, *minatorius*, from *minat-*: threatened, from the Latin, *minari*: to threaten

e.g. The teacher tried to control the unruly pupils by wagging his finger in a **minatory** fashion

ministrations (pl. noun) = *(humorously formal in tone)* **the provision of care** from the Latin, *ministrare*: to wait upon, from *minister*: servant, from *minus*: less

e.g. I broke my toe playing rugby but, thanks to the nurse's tender **ministrations**, I was soon back on the pitch

mise en abyme

---

mise en abyme (noun) = **a self-reflective piece of art that contains one or more smaller images of itself** *('abyme' is pronounced 'abeeme') for full explanation, see box below*

e.g. The film *Inception* features some characters having a 'dream within a dream'; critics say this **mise en abyme** made for a confusing storyline

---

'mise en abyme' means, in French, 'placed into abyss', and literally refers to the visual experience of standing in (the abyss) between two mirrors, seeing an infinite reproduction of one's own image as a result.

It was French novelist André Gide who invented the term: Gide wrote a novel called The Counterfeiters, *which featured a character called Edouard who is writing a novel that is also called* The Counterfeiters.

Perhaps the most famous example of a 'mise en abyme' is in Hamlet, when the prince, Hamlet himself, asks some strolling players to act out on stage 'The Murder of Gonzago'. The action and characters in this piece being acted out mirror the murder of Hamlet's father in the main action, and Hamlet wants to bring out this parallel to provoke a reaction from the murderer, his uncle King Claudius, who is watching the play; Hamlet makes this ploy explicit when he says, 'the play's the thing wherein I'll catch the conscience of the king.' (Incidentally, Hamlet calls this new play The Mousetrap, *which is of course the title that Agatha Christie took centuries later, for her own long-running play.)*

---

mise en scène (set phrase) = *(of an event)* **the setting or surrounds** *(pronounced 'meese on sen')* from the French, *mise en scène*: setting on the stage

e.g. When the police found the body of Andrew Cunanan, days after he'd shot dead Gianni Versace in 1997, the **mise en scène** was a boat, with the body surrounded by C.S. Lewis books

Mittel-European (adj.) = **coming from Central Europe (but a Central Europe where it is Germany specifically that is the dominant force)** *(pronounced 'mit-l-oi-roh-pah-yan') for full explanation, see box below*

e.g. Most new restaurants opening today seem to subscribe to the same **Mittel-European** look of blanched floorboards and metal lampshades

---

'Mitteleuropa' means, in German, 'Central Europe'. The word not only has a geographical meaning, but also a political one, denoting a German plan adopted during World War I, to create a German-dominated Central European block (comprising modern-day Germany and its immediately surrounding neighbours, such as Austria and Poland).

In his work Mitteleuropa *(1915), German thinker Friedrich Naumann advocated Germany absorbing its neighbouring territories, so as to stabilise the region via German rule. Details of the plan included the expulsion of non-Germans from annexed states, which would then be used as a buffer between Germany and hostile Russia. Germany would, in this way, be able to compete with the British Empire for the role of the world's dominant power.*

So, using the term 'Mittel-European' is a bit like referring to 'Western Europe' or 'Eastern Europe': the phrase is more than just a geographical denotation because it has clear political overtones (with the phrase 'Mittel-European' evoking Germany's past desire to dominate – just as the label 'Eastern Europe' really stands for communism; and 'Western Europe', for capitalism and democracy). And when you describe a restaurant (for example) as 'Mittel-European', you are saying it looks like it comes from Central Europe, but you are also needlessly reminding your interlocutor of Germany's bellicose history.

---

to micturate (verb) = **(comically formal in tone) to urinate** from the Latin, *micturier:* to want to urinate (the desiderative of *meiere:* to urinate)

e.g. The corner of my cupboard is my kitten Glenn's preferred place to **micturate**

mondain (adj.) = **worldy; part of fashionable society**
(pronounced 'mon-<u>dah</u>') from the French, *mondain:* wordly; ultimately from the Latin, *mundanus:* belonging to the world, from *mundus:* the world

e.g. Marilyn Monroe's charm was built on her naïve wonderment, whereas Elizabeth Taylor's appeal rested on her **mondain** knowingness

monograph (noun) = **a detailed written study of one subject only** from the Latin, *monographus:* writer on a single species

e.g. The *Bluffer's Guide* books are a series of **monographs** on topics ranging from sex to hiking

monomania (noun) = **an obsession with one thing** *(pronounced 'mon-uh-<u>mey</u>-nee-uh')* from the Greek, *monos:* one + *mania:* madness, from *mainesthai:* to be mad

e.g. Kim Jong II had a **monomania** for khahki jumpsuits, which he would be seen sporting on most public occasions

to monster (verb) = *(informal in tone)* **to criticise severely** from the Latin, *monstrum:* a portent or a monster, from *monere:* to warn

e.g. Celebrities are used to an occasional **monstering** in the tabloids

mores (pl. noun) = **the characteristic customs of a group** *(pronounced '<u>mohr</u>-eyz')* from the Latin, *mos, mor-:* a custom

e.g. Autistic people often seem unaware of social **mores**

mortmain (noun) = **the oppressive influence of the past on the present** *(pronounced '<u>mawrt</u>-meyn')* *for full explanation, see box below*

e.g. To paraphrase writer Graham Greene, it's clear that memory levies a **mortmain** on human beings: for our past experiences inform our present behaviour

'mortmain' derives from the Latin, 'mortua manus', meaning 'dead hand' (a phrase that alludes to impersonal ownership – in fact, to an ownership so impersonal that it is as if a dead person is the owner).

It's this concept, of the dead exercising posthumous control over their property by dictating how it must be used (long after they have died) that informs the meaning of 'mortmain', which refers to the 'oppressive influence of the past'.

(Incidentally, in legal terminology, 'mortmain' is used to mean 'the status of lands held inalienably, i.e. in a non-transferable way, by a corporation'.)

mote (noun) = **the tiniest bit of a thing** *(pronounced 'moht')* from the Dutch, *mot*: dust

e.g. The sunlight flooded through the window, illuminating **motes** of dust in the air

moue (noun) = **a pout** *(conveying annoyance or disgust)* *(pronounced 'moo')* from the French, *moue*: lip

e.g. Some men are inexorably drawn to blondes who sport a permanent **moue** of resentment

mountebank (noun) = **a person who deceives others using charm** *(especially so as to take money off them)* *(pronounced 'moun-tuh-bank')* from the Italian, *monta in banco!*: climb onto the bench!; *this command in Italian was originally directed to a seller of dubious medicines, when the time had come for him to get up onto a bench and start addressing his audience of potential customers and dupes*

e.g. Grannies must be vigilant for **mountebank** builders, who take cash off them but then never start work

moral hazard

moral hazard (set phrase) = *(of a situation)* **taking too much risk because one knows one is guaranteed forgiveness if the risk-taking goes wrong** *for full explanation, see box below*

e.g. Bailing out the banks has created a **moral hazard**: now every banker knows that he can take huge risks, and the government will pick up the tab if it all goes to pot

---

The term 'moral hazard' – which started life in the 17th century – was widely used by English insurance companies in the late 19th century: if an insured party was deemed to be likely to defraud the insurance company, the insurance company would talk of a 'moral hazard' in doing business with such a client.

In the 1960s, the concept of moral hazard was the subject of renewed study by economists, and, at this point, stopped referring exclusively to the immoral behaviour of the involved parties.

Instead, the term assumed its current meaning, with economists using it to describe inefficiencies that can occur in a situation as a whole (rather than to signify any specific party involved in the situation, such as the dodgy insured parties mentioned above). Specifically, 'moral hazard' now denotes the concept of overly risky behaviour going unpunished (such as when bankers know any catastrophic consequences of their unscrupulous lending will be made good by the government). But it's the whole situation that is prone to 'moral hazard', rather than just the bankers.

---

to drift into the arms of Morpheus (set phrase) = **to go to sleep** *('Morpheus' is pronounced 'mawr-fee-uhs') for full explanation, see box below*

e.g. If you watch a long play in a stuffy theatre, you'll soon find yourself **drifting into the arms of Morpheus**

In Roman mythology, 'Morpheus' was the god of dreams and also the son of the god of sleep (who was called 'Hypnos').

Note that the word 'morphine' also derives from the god 'Morpheus' (because morphine, of course, induces sleep, and ultimately, dreams); and that 'hypnosis' also derives from the god 'Hypnos' because, when hypnotised, you're in a sleep-like state.

moxie (noun) = **force of character** *(pronounced 'mok-see')* for full explanation, see box below

e.g. In taking on and beating the party favourite Hilary Clinton to the Democratic Presidential nomination, Obama showed real **moxie**

The word 'moxie' started life as the brand name of a bitter-tasting, carbonated drink popular in Maine in the United States. The drink, caramel in colour, was first produced in 1876 as a patent medicine called 'Moxie Nerve Food', with its creator (Dr Augustin Thompson of Union, Maine) claiming that his beverage contained an extract from a rare, unnamed South American plant, purportedly discovered by a friend of his, a certain Lieutenant Moxie, who had been successfully using it for years to cure all his ailments.

With time, Dr Thompson added soda water to the formula and sold it in bottles and in bulk as a soda fountain syrup, marketing it as 'a delicious blend of bitter and sweet, a drink to satisfy everyone's taste'.

As the result of an extensive advertising campaign by the Moxie Beverage Company, the term 'moxie' entered the American language, with the meaning of 'courage, daring, and energy' – as in: 'This guy's got moxie!'

---

mnemonic (noun) = **a device – such as a rhyme – to aid the memory** *(pronounced 'ni-mon-ik')* from the Greek, *mnemonikos*: of the memory

e.g. The 'thirty days hath September' rhyme – to remember how many days are in each month – is perhaps the most famous **mnemonic** in the world

mullioned (adj.) = **(of a window) having vertical bars going down** *(pronounced 'muhl-yuhnd')* from the Anglo–French, *moienel*: middle (presumably referring to the light in the middle, between each mullion or vertical bar)

e.g. From their **mullioned** eyries overlooking the dreaming spires, Oxford University professors give tutorials to privileged undergraduates

multivalent

multivalent (adj.) = **having many meanings** (*pronounced 'muhl-tiv-uh-luhnt'*) from the Latin, *multis*: many + *valentia*: power

e.g. Atheists say that the word 'God' is such a **multivalent** term that it's ceased to have any meaning

mutatis mutandis (adv.) = *(of a comparison between two or more things)* **with respective differences taken into consideration** (*pronounced 'moo-tatis moo-tandis'*) from the Latin, *mutatis mutandis*: things being changed that have to be changed

e.g. If teaching methods can be improved in US schools using particular techniques, then there's no reason these same methods cannot work, **mutatis mutandis**, in UK schools too

myrmidon (noun) = **a loyal follower who executes cruel orders without pity** (*pronounced 'mur-mi-don'*) *for full explanation, see box below*

e.g. Celebrities live in fear of tabloid newspaper owners and their **myrmidons**

The Myrmidons were a legendary people from Greek history, the fiercest warriors in the whole of Greece, known for their skill in battle and loyalty to their leaders. They were commanded by Achilles, as described in Homer's Iliad (c. 800 BC).

The Myrmidons were from good stock; their eponymous ancestor Myrmidon, a king of Thessalian Phthia, was the son of Zeus (and of Eurymedousa, a mortal princess of Phthia, who was seduced by Zeus in the form of an ant).

Nowadays, when we use the term 'myrmidon', we allude to the brusque efficiency of these warriors, but also to their fierceness in battle, for the phrase has the negative connotation of 'one who follows his orders without pity for his victim'.

---

nacreous (adj.) = **mother-of-pearl in colour** *(pronounced 'nak-ree-uhs')* from the Middle French, *nacre:* the type of shellfish that produces mother-of-pearl; and ultimately from the Arabic, *naqur:* hunting horn (which evokes the shape of the mother-of-pearl-coloured mollusk shell)

e.g. When you fry chopped onions with some butter, the onions soon turn **nacreous**

nebbish (noun) = **a pathetically weak man** from the Yiddish, *nebekh:* poor thing

e.g. Woody Allen's films often feature a **nebbish** who's involved with two women, neither of whom he can bring himself to leave

necromancer (noun) = **one who can predict the future because they practise black magic** *(pronounced 'nek-ruh-man-ser')* from the Greek, *nekromanteia:* divination from an exhumed corpse, from *nekros:* dead body + *manteia:* divination; *necromancy literally means 'one who claims to predict the future by communicating with the dead'*

e.g. John D. Rockefeller (1839–1937) was the first American to be worth $1bn because of his extraordinary powers of prediction: it was as if the man was a **necromancer**

necropolis (noun) = **a large cemetery** *(pronounced 'nuh-krop-uh-lis')* from the Greek, *nekros:* dead person + *polis:* city

e.g. Paris has a **necropolis** called the *Cimetière du Montparnasse* that contains the tombs of such luminaries as Jean-Paul Sartre, on whose gravestone tourists leave fresh, unlit cigarettes daily (apparently for the dead author's consumption)

noir

noir (adj.) = *(of a novel or film)* **featuring a crime story peppered with sex and violence, and containing a cynical and self-destructive detective (who is often an amateur)** *for full explanation, see box below*

e.g. The most famous recent example of **noir** fiction is *The Girl with The Dragon Tattoo*, which features an amateur detective investigating grimly violent murders, and enjoying multiple sexual relations; the novel was also made into a film **noir**

'noir' is a term used in just two phrases: 'noir fiction' (to describe a certain kind of crime novel) and 'film noir' (denoting a particular film genre). The term was first applied to American films in the mid-1940s by observers in France, who described such bleak films as being 'noir' (meaning, of course, 'black' in French).

To qualify for the term 'noir', a plot must revolve around a crime, and feature a self-destructive and cynical protagonist. Sex also looms large in the plot. If there is an investigator, he is invariably a 'man on the street', and not a professional detective; and he is usually linked to the crime, via a blood relation, for example.

James M. Cain remains the most famous exponent of the genre. His first novel, The Postman Always Rings Twice *(1934), is still cited as the leading example of both noir fiction and film noir (the book was turned into celluloid in 1946). Just 100 pages long, the story concerns a drifter who falls in love with a married woman. They kill her husband and get away with it; but then the woman dies in a car accident and the police wrongly convict her lover of her murder.*

---

nom de guerre (set phrase) = **an assumed name under which a person takes part in some form of activity, such as war or business** *(pronounced 'nom duh ger') for full explanation, see box opposite*

e.g. Sid Vicious (1957–79), bassist for *The Sex Pistols*, was in fact born with the name John Simon Ritchie; but when a hamster called Sid bit him, forcing him to exclaim, 'Sid is really vicious!', he became known by the **nom de guerre** Sid Vicious

'nom de guerre' is the French for 'war name'; in Ancien Régime France (c. 1400–1700), a new recruit to the army was given a 'nom de guerre' as a form of identification (as identification numbers hadn't yet been invented). For example, a man known for his prodigious liquor consumption would have the following as his 'nom de guerre': 'prêt-à-boire' (meaning 'ready to drink'). Soon these aliases replaced the men's real family names.

Later, in World War II, French Resistance fighters also adopted a 'nom de guerre', so that, if captured by the Nazis, it would be impossible to work out their surname, and there would, therefore, be no reprisal against their families. For the same reason, SAS soldiers still make use of a 'nom de guerre' today.

(Incidentally, the other reason to use a 'nom de guerre' as a soldier, was that, being called by a different name to the one you use at home, ensured you were divorced from domestic life when in your military frame of mind.)

nonpareil

nonpareil (adj.) *(usually placed after noun)* = **unrivalled**
(pronounced 'non-puh-<u>rel</u>') from the French, non-: not + pareil: equal,
ultimately from the Latin, par: equal

e.g. Steve Jobs is generally agreed to have been an innovator
nonpareil

nonplussed (adj.) = *(of a person)* **so surprised that they are
unsure how to react** for full explanation, see box below

e.g. If, rushing through Soho on the way to the theatre, you're
accosted by an individual offering you a 'special massage', you're
likely to feel a little **nonplussed**

---

*'nonplussed' derives from the Latin 'non plus': 'not more'; 'to
nonplus' means 'to bring someone to a state of nonplus', and
therefore, 'to make someone feel like they can do nothing more
(because of their shock)', and, hence, 'to perplex someone'.*

*But in recent years, a new meaning has started up in the United
States, with 'nonplussed' beginning to mean 'unperturbed'. This is
the exact opposite of its original meaning – and both meanings
are fighting it out.*

*So, if you choose to use the word 'nonplussed', no one can be sure
what you actually mean (as you could mean one of two
completely opposed things: this new meaning is the antithesis of
the first one). The best thing is perhaps to avoid using the word
'nonplussed' altogether, and simply to use instead the word
'bemused', if you're confused by a sudden happening – and the
word 'unperturbed' if you're inured to this same happening.*

---

normalcy (noun) = **the usual state of affairs;**
*note that 'normalcy' is just a fancy way of saying
'normality'* derived from the word normal;
normalcy has been associated since 1920 with US
President Warren G. Harding, who was prone to
linguistic gaffes – such as saying 'normalcy' when
he meant to say 'normality'

e.g. Pavarotti's funeral was so significant in Italy
that it was broadcast live on CNN: it was days
before the population calmed down and
normalcy was restored

notwithstanding (preposition; usually placed after the noun)
= **in spite of** *an expression adopted by English from the Latin: a literal translation of the Latin phrase, 'non obstante' which means 'being no hindrance'*

e.g. Frequent rows **notwithstanding**, theirs was a happy marriage

nugatory (adj.) = **of no importance** *(pronounced 'nyoo-guh-tawr-ee')* from the Latin, *nugatorius*, from *nugari*: to trifle, from *nugae*: jests

e.g. Kim Jong Il behaved as if the United State's threats to his nation were **nugatory**

to pay obeisance to (someone) (set phrase) = **to pay homage to (someone), often by bowing** *('obeisance' is pronounced 'oh-bey-suhns') for full explanation, see box below*

e.g. By staging street parties to commemorate her Diamond Jubilee, the British people **paid obeisance to** the Queen

---

'obeisance' is from the Old French, 'obeissance', itself from 'obeissant': 'an act of obeying', the present participle of 'obeir': 'to obey'.

But how did the concept of obeying someone come to be associated with the bow – or any other gesture of deference – implied by the English term 'obeisance'? After all, just because you're obeying someone doesn't mean you have to drop to your knee whilst doing so.

Well, the sense of 'obeisance' in English altered in the late 14th century from 'obeying' to 'a bending of the body in homage, often by bowing' because the French word 'obeissance' was itself being confused at that time with the Old French 'abaisance', meaning 'the lowering of oneself' (altering the meaning of its English counterpart in the same way). And this is the reason why the verb 'to pay obeisance to someone' today means 'to produce a gesture of submission, such as a bow (or a street party, in the case of a Diamond Jubilee), to show homage'.

---

objective correlative (set phrase) = *(of art)* a situation or object designed to evoke a particular emotion in the audience
('correlative' is pronounced 'kuh-rel-uh-tiv') for full explanation, see box below

e.g. To evoke sadness, a skilled film director won't have a character say, 'I'm sad', but instead will film an **objective correlative** such as rain falling

The theory of the 'objective correlative' was developed by the poet T.S. Eliot (1888–1965), whose most famous poem, written in 1922, is 'The Waste Land' (a work with an unclear meaning but which nevertheless succeeds in evoking the soulless atmosphere after World War I). In one essay, Eliot advocated the 'objective correlative' as a means of revealing the emotions of a character (in a novel) implicitly, via the use of a physical image – rather than explicitly, by some wordy description. Eliot wrote,

'The only way of expressing emotion in the form of art is by finding an "objective correlative"; in other words, a set of objects, a situation, a chain of events which shall be the formula of that particular emotion; such that when the external facts, which must terminate in sensory experience, are given, the emotion is immediately evoked.'

Two obvious examples of an 'objective correlative' are – in a film or in a book – a storm (to convey turbulent emotions), or a scorching desert (to exemplify aridity of feeling).

obloquy (noun) = **vitriol** *(pronounced 'ob-luh-kwee')* from the Latin, *obloquy*, from *ob-*: against + *loqui*: to speak

e.g. After allegations of child abuse were levelled against him, Michael Jackson endured years of public **obloquy**

obsequies (pl. noun) = **funeral rites** *(pronounced 'ob-si-kwees')* from the medieval Latin (plural), *obsequiae*, from the Latin, *exsequiae*: funeral rites, along the lines of *obsequium*: dutiful service

e.g. The Untied Kingdom went into mass mourning during the **obsequies** of Diana, Princess of Wales

(the) obverse (of)

(the) obverse (of) (noun) = *(within an argument)* **the related matter (to)** *for full explanation, see box below*

e.g. Tabloid journalists argue that uncovering a proper scandal that can affect a nation (such as the Bill Clinton / Monica Lewinsky case) is simply the **obverse** of investigating the private lives of every celebrity out there, which is why the latter must never be banned

---

'obverse' comes from the Latin, 'obvertere': 'to turn toward', from 'ob-': 'toward' + 'vertere': 'to turn'. 'The obverse' of a coin is the 'other side' or the 'reverse' side of the coin. (The 'obverse' side is often known as 'heads', because it usually displays the head of a famous person such as the Queen; and the 'reverse' side is 'tails'.)

But of course both sides are on the same coin – and this is important, because the 'obverse of a fact' is a 'related matter to this fact' (i.e. a part of this fact, just as surely as the 'obverse' side of a coin is a part of the coin); but note that the 'obverse' of a fact is not necessarily 'the opposite of this fact' (although it can be the 'opposite of a fact' – in the sense that 'the opposite' of a fact is of course still related, albeit in a negative way, to the fact).

Examples include: 'The obverse of my unstinting cynicism is my occasional lurch into sentimentality – as a kind of safety valve'; and, 'His deteriorating career was the obverse of his busier love life'.

---

occulted (adj.) = **hidden** *(pronounced 'uh-kuhlt-ed')* from the Latin, *occultus*: hidden, from *occulere*: to conceal, from *ob-*: over + *(a verb related to) celare*: to hide; the meaning of 'hidden from the mind, beyond human understanding' is from the 1540s, and supernatural connotations are from the 1630s

e.g. The sun was **occulted** by threatening clouds

occluded (adj.) = **closed off** *(pronounced 'uh-klood-ed')* from the Latin, *occludere*: to close up, from *ob-*: up + *claudere*: to close

e.g. In the film *Tinker, Tailor, Soldier, Spy*, the **occluded** atmosphere of life in the British secret service is well conveyed

to apply Ockham's razor to (a problem) (set phrase) = **to take the view that the simplest explanation (to a problem) is usually the correct one** *for full explanation, see box opposite*

to apply Ockham's razor to (a problem)

e.g. The doctor dismissed my own hypochondriacal explanation for my symptoms and instead **applied Ockham's razor to** my case, saying, 'It's just the flu that's going around'

William of Ockham was a friar who lived in Ockham, Surrey, between 1285 and 1349. A great scholar, he recommended minimalism in thought processes – based on the fact that nature usually uses the simplest means to an end, so, to work out an explanation for a natural phenomenon (or 'get into the mind of Nature'), it's best to ape this simplicity in your own thought processes. The phrase summing up this system is 'Ockham's razor', which holds that, when confronted with a variety of competing explanations, you should always go for the simplest explanation. (The word 'razor' is incorporated into the phrase because it's by 'shaving away' overly elaborate theories, that you arrive at the correct theory.) Most TV detectives seem to apply this principle – even if they don't credit Ockham – when they explain how they worked out that it was the butler who was the murderer, by admitting, 'It was the simplest explanation'.

Although Ockham was obsessed with finding the simplest explanation for a phenomenon, he was also insistent on finding supporting evidence, too. Therefore, a more simple explanation with no evidence behind it – such as 'the little leprechauns did it' – is trumped by a less simple explanation which <u>does</u> have supporting facts behind it. In practice, Ockham's theory works sometimes, but not always. For example, applying Ockham's razor meant scientists incorrectly rejected DNA as the carrier of genetic information in favour of proteins, since the latter initially appeared to be a simpler, more elegant explanation as a vessel for DNA (but of course this was still the wrong explanation in the end, confounding Ockham's theory). On the other hand, biologists have found it useful to apply Ockham's razor to explain altruism amongst animals, which biologists have decided is based, very simply, on an individual's desire to protect his own genes – by protecting his offspring, who carry these genes – rather than being based on an (allegedly) 'more complicated' explanation (such as mankind being endowed with a God-given altruistic streak).

*The main problem with Ockham's theory is that we are all subjective beings, and a theory that is compatible with one person's world view will be deemed (attractively) 'simple' by that person, but (unattractively) 'complex' by someone with a different subjective view. Hence Ockham's razor can be seen as just a 'mirror of prejudice', or a **Rorschach test** (see later entry in this book).*

odalisque (noun) = **a sexually attractive woman** (*pronounced 'ohd-ul-isk'*) from the Turkish, *odalik*, from *oda*: chamber + *lik*: function; *an 'odalisque' literally means 'a female slave in a harem'*

e.g. Model Sophie Dahl is a big fan of the painter Matisse, exclaiming, 'He can make even a jug joyful and sensuous, and his **odalisques** are heaven'

oenophile (adj.) = **someone who is a connoisseur of wines** (*pronounced 'ee-no-file'*) from the Greek, *oinos*: wine + *philos*: loving, from *philein: to love; note the term was only invented in the 1930s, so something less Greek – and less pretentious – could easily have been chosen (but then wine lovers do, endearingly, often go in for Greek-style, highfalutin' terminology)*

e.g. At the wedding dinner, the Pauillac wine that was served with the beef was an **oenophile**'s delight

ontological (adj.) = **concerning the subject of existence itself** from the Greek, *ontologia*, from the Greek, *on, ont-*: being + *logos*: the study (of)

e.g. In his teenage years, he spent hours locked in his bedroom, contemplating questions such as 'How do we know we exist?' and other **ontological** brainteasers

opalescent (adj.) = **showing varying colours** (*pronounced 'oh-puh-les-uhnt'*) *'opalescent' derives from the word 'opal', a gemstone that shows varying colours when placed against the ground*

e.g. When Margaret Thatcher was driven from 10 Downing Street for the last time in 1990, waiting photographers captured – through the glass of her car window – the **opalescent** tears in her eyes

oracular (adj.) = **(of someone's words) mysterious** (*pronounced 'aw-rak-yuh-ler'*) from the Latin, *oraculum*: an oracle, from *orare*: to speak

e.g. Towards the end of his career, Eric Cantona seemed to cultivate an **oracular** style, answering questions from the press with allusions to seagulls and sardines

ossified (adj.) = **stagnant** from the French, *ossifier*, from the Latin, *os, oss-*: bone; *'ossified' literally means 'to have changed into hard bone', i.e. 'rigid' (and hence, metaphorically speaking, 'stagnant')*

e.g. Critics say the Royal Family is an **ossified** institution well past its 'sell by' date

otiose (adj.) = **of no use** *(pronounced 'oh-tee-ohs')* from the Latin, *otiosus:* not busy, from *otium:* leisure; *'otiose' literally means 'not busy', and from there, it's a short hop to the current metaphorical sense, 'of no use'*

e.g. So that his colleagues should think him a 'team player', he attended the meeting and amused himself with the purposefully **otiose** point he contributed to the group discussion, just so no one could deny his attendance later

oubliette (noun) = **a place hidden away** *(pronounced 'oo-blee-et')* from the French, *oublier:* to forget; *an 'oubliette' literally refers to 'a secret dungeon, only accessible via a trapdoor in its ceiling' (and hence to 'a place so inconspicuous that it has been forgotten about')*

e.g. As soon as their retirement starts, men often seem to vanish into an **oubliette** of daytime TV viewing

overweening (adj.) = **immoderate** from the present participle of the Middle English, *overwenen:* to be over-confident, from the Old English, *ofer-wenian*, from *ofer*: over + *wenian*: to think (giving the sense of 'thinking too much of oneself, immoderate')

e.g. Richard Nixon's **overweening** presumptuousness led him to tap every White House phone conversation without his interlocutor's permission

pabulum (noun) = **trite words** (*pronounced 'pab-yuh-luhm'*) for *full explanation, see box below*

e.g. Readers lap up the **pabulum** of self-help books, such as those explaining how the perfect relationship can be yours

---

'pabulum' derives from the Latin word 'pabulum', meaning 'food'. The negative tones of the current usage were born in 1932, when the Mead Johnson Company gave the name 'Pablum' (a contracted form of 'pabulum') to a bland cereal that was a food for babies.

Forty or so years later, in 1970, US Vice President Spiro Agnew used the term to refer to 'mushy' political prose, and the damaging connotations – of 'bland intellectual nourishment' and hence 'trite words' – have stuck ever since.

Incidentally, all of this negativity surrounding the word (and the cereal, by implication) is a bit unfair, because 'Pablum' (the cereal) – although it may have tasted bland – was a great help to millions of children, providing them with vital vitamin D that stopped the rickets epidemic in its tracks. But let's not focus on the good points here: the word 'pabulum' is now a defamatory one, unfairly or not.

---

pace (+ 'name of person') (preposition) = **with all due respect to (+'name of person')** (*pronounced 'pah-chey'*) from the Latin, *pace*: in peace, as in the Latin, *pace tua*: by your leave; *note that a phrase starting with 'pace' is always an aside that contradicts the rest of the sentence*

e.g. Matt Damon is married to an ex-bartender; Michelle Pfeiffer is the spouse of a screenwriter: in general, Hollywood stars, **pace** Brad and Angelina, rarely marry other Hollywood stars

(a) paean to (something) (noun) = **a eulogy about (something)** (*pronounced 'pee-uhn'*) from the Greek, *paian*: a hymn of thanksgiving to Paian, the Greek god of healing (also known by his more famous name of Apollo, god of medicine)

e.g. Obama's inaugural speech was a **paean to** American optimism

(a) paladin of (a cause) (noun) = (a) defender of (a cause)
(pronounced 'pal-uh-din') for full explanation, see box below

e.g. After his death, it became clear that JFK was not the **paladin of** family values that he appeared to be, and had in fact been conducting numerous extra-marital affairs

---

'paladin' derives from the Middle French, 'paladin', meaning 'a warrior', itself ultimately originating from the Latin, 'palatinus', a 'palace official'.

The concept of the noble fighter known as the 'paladin' is immortalised in the oldest surviving major work of French literature, The Song of Roland *(c. 1150), (or La Chanson de Roland, as it's known in French). In this work, a 'paladin' referred to each of the 12 foremost warriors who protected King Charlemagne (742–814), whose bold invasions and Christian proselytising made him the first Emperor of Western Europe since the fall of the Roman Empire 400 years previously. In* The Song of Roland, *these 12 paladins of Charlemagne's stood for Christian valour in the King's battle against the Saracen hordes (which we'd call 'Arab tribes' today).*

Although King Charlemagne certainly existed, there is actually zero evidence the paladins ever did (outside of literature). Yet these fictitious fighters' bravery lives on in the word 'paladin', which continues to denote a stalwart defender of a cause.

---

paleontologist (noun) = a hunter for prehistoric fossils *(used – doubtless unfairly – as shorthand for someone uninteresting)*
(pronounced 'pal-ee-uhn-tol-uh-jist') from the Greek, *palaio-*: ancient + *ontos*: being + *logos*: the study (of)

e.g. His wife loved to mock him, telling him his prized collection of rare first edition Dickens novels would only be of interest to **palaeontologists**

(a) panegyric (on) (a subject) (noun) = a eulogy about (a subject) *(pronounced 'pan-i-jir-ik')* from the Greek, *panegyrikos (logos)*: (a speech) given in a public assembly in honour of a god, from *pan*: all + *agyris*: place of assembly

e.g. The film *Pretty Woman* is really **a panegyric on** all-conquering love

135

(a) panjandrum (of) (a professional field)

(a) panjandrum (of) (a professional field) = a pompous
powerful person within (a professional field) *(pronounced
'pan-jan-druhm') for full explanation, see box below*

e.g. Her first novel was snapped up because her father was a
panjandrum of the publishing business

---

*The story behind how the word 'panjandrum' came to be, is
bizarre and shows just how random the business of etymology is.
For 'panjandrum' is a word invented on the spur of the moment,
for a literary contest. The contest in question was proposed in
1753 by an actor called Charles Macklin, who claimed – at a public
lecture he gave in Covent Garden, London – that his memory was
so vast that he could remember any text after just one reading.
Hoping to catch him out, a playwright present called Samuel
Foote asked the lecturer to repeat the following verse of nonsense
(that Foote had composed on the spot, and proceeded to declaim):*

*'So she went into the garden to cut a cabbage-leaf to make an
apple pie; and at the same time a great she-bear, coming up the
street, pops its head into the shop. "What! No soap?" So he died,
and she very imprudently married the barber; and there were
present the Picninnies, and the Joblillies, and the Garyulies, and
the grand Panjandrum himself, with the little round button at the
top, and they all fell to playing the game of catch as catch can till
the gunpowder ran out at the heels of their boots.'*

*So irritated was Macklin by this burst of nonsense, that he refused
to repeat it, and officially lost at his own challenge of memory feat.
And of all the words in the paragraph above (that came out of
Samuel Foote's mouth), it's only 'panjandrum' that survives today,
and it continues to carry the sense of a 'pompous powerful person'.*

(a) pastiche (of) (something) (noun) = *(of art)* a work that is a blend of previous works; *note that a 'pastiche' is usually a respectful homage to the works it references, whereas a 'parody' is a comic exaggeration of the work it evokes* from the Italian, *pasticcio*: piecrust (which is of course made up of a blend of flour, fat, liquid and salt, all mixed together – just as surely as a 'pastiche' is itself a blend), ultimately from the Latin, *pasta*: paste

e.g. *The House of Silk*, a recent Sherlock Holmes novel written by Anthony Horowitz, is the first ever Holmes **pastiche** to be endorsed by the Sir Arthur Conan Doyle estate

patrimony (noun) = **heritage** *(pronounced 'pa-truh-moh-nee')* from the French, *patrimoine*, from the Latin, *patrimonium*, from *pater*: father; *often 'patrimony' refers specifically to property inherited from one's father*

e.g. During the Egyptian Revolution of 2011, the Egyptian Museum of Antiquities – which contains such treasures as King Tutankhamun's Gold Mask and other vital cultural **patrimony** – was broken into, and two mummies reportedly destroyed

paucity (noun) = **scarcity** *(pronounced 'paw-si-tee')* from the Latin, *paucitas*: scarcity, from *paucus*: few

e.g. People want something light for their holiday, so airport bookshops contain a multitude of paperback thrillers, but a **paucity** of more serious literature

peaceable (adj.) = *(of a person)* promoting **calm** *(pronounced 'pee-suh-buhl')* from the Old French, *paisible*: peaceable, from *pais*: peace, ultimately from the Latin, *pax, pacis*: peace

e.g. He avoided confrontations like the plague, for he was a **peaceable** type

pedagogic (adj.) = **relating to teaching**; *note that, when used of a person, the tone is derogatory, in the sense of 'haughty like a teacher'* (*pronounced 'ped-uh-goj-ik'*) *from the Old French, pedagogue: teacher of children, from the Greek, paidagogos: slave who escorted children to school, from pais, paidos: child + agogos: leader*

e.g. Fed chairman Ben Bernanke once taught economics at Princeton University, and critics say that when he briefs journalists nowadays about the outlook for the US economy, he continues to emit a **pedagogic** air

penumbra (noun) = **a surrounding area** (*pronounced 'pen-uhm-bruh'*) *from the Latin, paene: almost + umbra: shadow; a 'penumbra' literally means 'the partially shaded area around the edges of a shadow, where the shade blends into light (with the gradation being almost imperceptible)'*

e.g. From out of the London riots – which originally started as a protest against perceived police brutality – spread a large **penumbra** of opportunistic looting and violence

peon (noun) = **an unskilled worker** (*pronounced 'pee-uhn'*) *from the Spanish, peon, ultimately from the medieval Latin, pedo, pedon-: foot soldier, from the Latin, pes, ped-: foot; 'peon' originally referred to an unskilled Spanish-American farmworker*

e.g. Astronauts aren't exactly normal nine-to-five **peons**

periphrastic (adj.) = **speaking in a roundabout way** (*pronounced 'per-uh-fras-tik'*) *from the Greek, periphrazein: to declare in a roundabout way, from peri-: round about + phrazein: to express*

e.g. When a politician wants to avoid answering an interviewer's question, he becomes even more **periphrastic** than usual

to pernoctate (in a place) (verb) = *(formal in tone)* **to pass the night (in a place)** *from the Latin, pernoctare: to spend the night, from per-: through + nox, noctis: night*

e.g. It was only after she married him that she allowed herself to **pernoctate** in his flat

perquisite (noun) = **a perk (of one's position)** *(pronounced 'pur-kwuh-zit')* from the Latin, *perquisitum*: something gained, from *perquirere*: to search diligently, from *per-*: thoroughly + *quaerere*: to seek; *'perk' is simply the abbreviated form of 'perquisite'*

e.g. The US President enjoys numerous **perquisites** of office, such as regularly dining with Hollywood stars

persiflage (noun) = **light teasing** *(pronounced 'pur-suh-flarge')* from the French, *persifler*: to banter, originally from *siffler*: to whistle, itself deriving from the Latin, *sibilare*: to hiss

e.g. Usually it is a spirit of **persiflage** that dominates TV debates between politicians, but sometimes this can spill over into angry shouting matches

pertinacious (adj.) = **very obstinate** *(pronounced 'pur-tin-ey-shuhs')* from the Latin, *pertinax*, *pertinaci-*: holding fast

e.g. She felt zero attraction towards him, but he was such a **pertinacious** suitor that eventually she gave in to his requests for a date

a Petri dish (for nourishing something)
(set phrase) = **a breeding ground (for nourishing something)** *for full explanation, see box below*

e.g. Numerous cases of cocaine addiction amongst bankers have shown that a life of stress is the perfect **Petri dish** for nourishing drug addiction

---

A 'Petri dish' is a shallow glass dish – with a loose-fitting cover – that scientists use as a breeding ground for bacteria (thus making it possible for them to identify those bacteria that are responsible for disease).

It is named after its inventor, German bacteriologist Julius Richard Petri (1852–1922). Today the term 'Petri dish' is used metaphorically to describe any breeding ground.

---

pheromones (pl. noun) = **vibes;** *literally meaning 'chemicals released into the environment by an animal, affecting the behaviour of other animals'* (pronounced 'fer-uh-mohns') from the Greek, *pherein*: to carry + the English word *hormone*, from the Greek, *hormon*, present participle of *horman*: to set in motion *(the word 'pheronome' was invented in 1959)*

e.g. People who are already in a relationship are much more attractive to others, for there is no bigger aphrodisiac than giving out spoken-for **pheromones**

philippic (against something) (noun) = **a tirade (against something)** *(pronounced 'fi-lip-ik') for full explanation, see box below*

e.g. The journalist penned a **philippic** against her cheating husband that was published nationwide the next day

---

The word 'philippic' originated with Demosthenes (384–322 BC), a Greek orator who – from his base in Athens – delivered several verbal attacks on Philip II of Macedon. At the time of Demosthenes' attack, Macedon was just a small, relatively unthreatening-looking kingdom situated on the Greek peninsula; but Demosthenes correctly sensed that Philip II of Macedon was about to hugely expand his kingdom via acts of aggression that would threaten Athens.

So Demosthenes urged his fellow Greeks to unite and fight against King Philip, to neutralise this threat while it was still possible to do so. These series of speeches against Philip were known as the 'philippics'. But Demosthenes failed to sufficiently galvanise his audience, who did not heed his warnings; and eventually Philip's son Alexander the Great – confirming Demosthenes' hunch – became one of the greatest conquerors of all time, sweeping away all before him (including Demosthenes' complacent audience). As for Demosthenes himself, he was hunted down by Alexander's men and ended up committing suicide in order to evade capture.

Demosthenes' speeches – which were a failure (in the sense that the audience was not roused into action) – have nevertheless become immortalised in our language as meaning a 'tirade'.

(a) piety (noun) = **a platitude** *(pronounced 'pahy-i-tee')* from the Old French, *piete*, from the Latin, *pietas*: dutiful conduct

e.g. When an actor wins an Oscar, his acceptance speech usually includes a 'thank you' to his parents for being so supportive, and other such **pieties**

pinguid (adj.) = **fat, oily** *(pronounced 'ping-wid')* from the Latin, *pinguis*: fat

e.g. If a **pinguid** man is forced to take the stairs rather than a lift, much wheezing will result

plebiscite (noun) = **a referendum** *(pronounced 'pleb-uh-sit')* from the Latin, *plebiscitum*: a decree of the people, from *plebs, pleb-*: the common people + *scitum*: decree, from *sciscere*: to vote for

e.g. In the aftermath of World War I, a number of **plebiscites** were held, to decide on geographical boundaries within Europe

plenary (adj.) = *(of a big meeting)* **fully attended by all committee members** *(pronounced 'plen-uh-ree')* from the late Latin, *plenarius*: complete, from *plenus*: full

e.g. If Russia threatened to bomb the United Kingdom, doubtless the Prime Minister would call a **plenary** session of the cabinet

plenipotentiary (noun) = **a diplomat fully authorised to represent his government** *(pronounced 'plen-uh-puh-ten-shuh-ree')* from the Medieval Latin, *plenipotentiarius*: having full power, from *plenus*: full + *potentem*: powerful

e.g. When international rock stars visit London, they tend to hire entire floors of luxury hotels: it is as if some **plenipotentiary** has come to town

pleonastic (adj.) = *(of a person)* **using too many words**
(*pronounced '<u>play</u>-uh-nas-tic'*) from the Greek, *pleonazein*: to be
superfluous

e.g. An expression like 'very unique' is **pleonastic**, for you can
easily drop the 'very' altogether

pliant (adj.) = **compliant** (*pronounced '<u>plahy</u>-uhnt'*) from the Old
French, *pliant*: bending, the present participle of *plier*: to bend; *from
here, the figurative sense of 'easily influenced, compliant' developed*

e.g. In the film *Black Swan*, Natalie Portman plays a young
ballerina, who is initially a **pliant** daughter, but who soon becomes
impossible to control

plosive (noun) = **a sound produced when saying out loud a consonant – either d, b, g, t, k, or p – that requires stopping the airflow at some point, then suddenly releasing it, such as the sound 'd' in 'dog'** *(pronounced 'ploh-siv')* plosive is a shortened version of the word *explosive*

e.g. 'Tulip', with its 't' and 'p', is a **plosive**-heavy word

pogrom (noun) = **the government-organised massacre of one ethnic group, often the Jews** *(pronounced 'poh-gruhm')* for full explanation, see box below

e.g. When President Obama nominated two liberal law professors to senior posts, critics said this constituted a **pogrom** against Christians. But these critics were, in their turn, lambasted for using the word 'pogrom' too lightly

---

'pogrom' is the Russian word for 'devastation', originally deriving from 'po': 'through' and 'gromu': 'thunder'; it is fitting that the word is Russian in origin, for the first pogrom was in Russia, with the Jews being the ethnic group targeted.

More specifically, the first such massacre to be labelled a pogrom took place in 1881–84, and involved the killing of Jews and the destruction of Jewish homes, businesses and synagogues; all of this was allegedly condoned by Russian law enforcement. The trigger for these assaults was the assassination of Tsar Alexander II in 1881, which many blamed on 'the Jews'. (But in actual fact, none of the bombers was Jewish and their only vague semitic link was that a close associate of theirs was a Jewish woman.) Following these atrocities, many other pogroms against Jews took place in Russia; but of course the most horrendous examples occurred in Nazi Germany.

'pogrom' can also refer to the extermination of non-Jews; for example, since the US invasion of Iraq in 2003, Iraqi Christians – which make up just 5 per cent of the total population – have experienced many massacres (often referred to as 'pogroms') at the hands of their compatriots.

Today the term 'pogrom' is applied to any such genocide and it remains a highly emotive word, recalling as it does so many prior killings in history. So charged is the term that people frequently object when it is used, complaining that it's being employed too lightly, and should be reserved only to describe awful massacres involving a huge loss of life.

poltroon (noun) = **a total coward** (*pronounced 'pol-troon'*) from the Medieval French, *poultron:* a coward, ultimately from the Italian, *poltrone*: coward, idler; from *poltro*: bed

e.g. Hit-and-run drivers are the worst kind of **poltroon**

Pooh-bah (noun) = **a pompous official who holds many fatuous titles** *for full explanation, see box below*

e.g. Whenever the stockmarket plunges, there's usually a gathering of international **Pooh-bahs** who hold a conference to try and shore up investors' confidence

'Pooh-bah' was the title of a character in The Mikado *(1885). In this comic opera – set far away from Britain, in Japan, so as to allow Gilbert and Sullivan more freedom to satirise British politics – 'Pooh-bah' holds many preposterous titles, including 'First Lord of the Treasury, Lord Chief Justice, Commander-in-Chief, Lord High Admiral...Archbishop of Titipu, Lord Mayor, and Lord High Everything Else'.*

The name 'Pooh-bah' is thus now used as a mocking title for someone – often a politician – who is self-important and who holds many irrelevant titles.

postmodernist (adj.) = *(of an artwork)* **reflecting the artist's belief that there is no such thing as progress, and that pessimism is the appropriate response to life (often shown via apocalyptic imagery)** *for full explanation, see box below*

e.g. On their date in the art gallery, he nodded sagely when she described the paintings as '**postmodernist**'; but he in fact had no idea what she was talking about, and, after spending an hour that evening researching the term, was still none the wiser

'postmodernism', a movement which has dominated the intellectual scene since the 1960s, is a reaction against the prior movement of 'modernism' – so, to understand 'postmodernism', it's essential to understand 'modernism'.

So, looking firstly at 'modernism': this was a movement lasting from around 1800 to 1960, and was marked by a loss of faith in all previously held certainties. In particular, Darwin's On the Origin of Species by Means of Natural Selection *(1852), as well as the horror of World War I (1914–18), led, for many, to the loss of religious belief, and consequently artists lost belief also in other 'traditions', such as the previously held role of art (which was to accurately depict reality). In its stead, 'modernism' substituted self-consciousness of artistic expression, leading to experiments with form and presentation – but to a total indifference towards content and meaning. Modernists regarded this innovation – this emphasis on form over content – as progress.*

As a reaction against 'modernism' (and its belief in progress, via the emphasis of form over content), 'postmodernism' holds that there is in fact no progress: modern society is not improving, nor is it superior to previous societies (no matter how much you play with form in the way the modernists did). Hence 'postmodernist' art often involves apocalyptic imagery and pessimism about life. Unfortunately part of this pessimism has spilt over into a loss of belief in the ability to define anything at all, including 'postmodernism' itself. In fact, in many ways, if you're so crass as to attempt to define 'postmodernism', then you 'just don't get it'. Understandably, as a result of all this, many have concluded the term 'postmodernist' is without meaning.

posthaste (adv.) = **with great speed** (pronounced 'pohst-heyst') *from the command, 'haste, post, haste', written on letters around 1530, to speed them on their way*

e.g. When she found out her sister was ill, she returned **posthaste** to England

to potentiate (an effect) (verb) = **to enhance (an effect)** *(pronounced 'puh-ten-shee-eight') from the Latin, potentia: power*

e.g. Many writers find that coffee **potentiates** the creative juices

predation (noun) = **the act of plundering** *(pronounced 'pre-dey-shuhn') from the Latin, praedatio-: the taking of booty, from the verb, praedari: to seize as plunder, from praeda: booty*

e.g. The Arab Spring began when thousands of people demonstrated against **predation** by state officials

preferment (noun) = **promotion** *(pronounced 'pri-fur-muhnt')* from the English words, *prefer-* + *ment*

e.g. After he spat in his boss's face, his chances of **preferment** collapsed

primacy (noun) = **dominance** *(pronounced 'pry-muh-see')* from the Latin, *primatia*: primacy, from the Latin, *primas, primat-*: of the first rank

e.g. Over the past decade, the **primacy** of Roger Federer in the world of tennis is clear

privations (pl. noun) = **the lack of the usual comforts of life (often owing to poverty)** *(pronounced 'pry-vey-shuhns')* from the Latin, *privatio*: deprivation, from the Latin, *privare*: to deprive

e.g. People on the poverty line regularly suffer from hunger and other **privations**

probity (noun) = **uprightness** *(pronounced 'pro-bi-tee')* from the Latin, *probitas*: goodness, from *probus*: good

e.g. He was praised for his **probity** in coming forward and reporting his colleague for embezzling

(a) profusion (of) (something) (noun) = **(a) large amount (of something)** *(pronounced 'pruh-fyoo-zhuhn')* from the Latin, *profusio*: a pouring out, from the Latin, *profundere*: to pour out

e.g. In spring, there is a **profusion of** colour as the trees blossom

prole (noun) = **a member of the working class** *(pronounced 'prohl')* for full explanation, see box below

e.g. Whereas a few decades ago, people in Britain would try to sound like an aristocrat to get ahead in the world, nowadays, in today's egalitarian society, they try to sound like a **prole** to achieve the same goal

---

The word 'prole' is an abbreviation of 'proletariat', which derives from the Latin, 'proletarius': 'member of the lowest class', itself based on 'proles': 'offspring' (because the Romans used the term 'proles' to denote a person who had no wealth in property, and who consequently paid no taxes, and therefore only really served the state by producing offspring).

Promethean (adj.) = **defiantly original** *(pronounced 'pro-mee-thee-uhn') for full explanation, see box below*

e.g. In 1996, investors in Apple rejoiced when – after an 11-year absence from the company – Steve Jobs, the irascible genius with the **Promethean** touch, returned

---

'Promethean' derives from the story of Prometheus, a highly intelligent – but controversial – god from Greek mythology.

It was Prometheus who had the gall to steal fire from under the nose of the king of the gods, Zeus himself, and share it with mankind. His method was defiantly original: Prometheus hid the fire away in the thick stalk of a giant fennel plant and made off with it. (Irked by this, Zeus punished mankind by sending the first woman, Pandora, to earth; the Greek poet Hesiod, writing in the 8th century BC, commented on her arrival thus, '...of her is the deadly race and tribe of women who live amongst mortal men to their great trouble, no helper in hateful poverty, but only in wealth', before proceeding in similar progressive tones.)

Zeus eventually caught up with Prometheus and, by way of revenge, chained Prometheus to a rock; then an eagle would come by each day, and eat out his liver. Overnight the liver would grow back, and the eagle would fly back the next morning, to start the process of torture afresh. Today, the defiant originality of Prometheus – specifically, the ingenious way in which he stole fire from Zeus – is recalled when we call a great innovator like Steve Jobs 'Promethean'.

---

to propitiate (someone) (verb) = **to appease (someone)**
(pronounced 'pro-pish-ee-eight') from the Latin, *propitiare*: to make favourable, from *propitius*: favourable

e.g. Even though he didn't find his boss's jokes funny, he made a point of laughing at them – purely so as to **propitiate** his senior ahead of bonus day

propinquity (noun) = **the state of being near (to someone or something)** *(pronounced 'pro-ping-kwi-tee')* from the Latin, *propinquitas*: propinquity, from *propinque*: near, from *prope*: near to

e.g. She opened her eyes after her nap and sensed her husband's **propinquity**

to proscribe (verb) = **to forbid** from the Latin, *proscribere*: to publish in writing (literally: 'to write in front of', from *pro-*: in front of + *scribere*: to write); *in time, this included the sense of 'to publish in writing the name of someone who is an outlaw (i.e. who has been forbidden)'*

e.g. Condoms are **proscribed** by the Catholic church

provenance (noun) = **the source** (*pronounced 'prov-uh-nuhns'*) from the Latin, *provenire*: to come forth, from *pro-*: forth + *venire*: to come

e.g. He asked to see the wine's label, and, after scanning the writing on it, expressed admiration at its St Julien **provenance**

pudenda (pl. noun) = **a woman's external genital organs** (*pronounced 'pyoo-den-da'*) from the Latin, *pudenda (membra)*: (parts) to be ashamed of, from *pudere*: to be ashamed

e.g. A certain kind of starlet – when getting out of a car – seems to get a kick from flashing her **pudenda** at the paparazzi

pudeur (noun) = **embarrassment about sex** (*pronounced 'poo-der'*) from the French, *pudeur*: modesty

e.g. She went into Stringfellows nightclub with the other traders; but then, as more and more G-string-clad women approached her, she was overcome by **pudeur** and fled

pulchritude (noun) = **beauty** (*pronounced 'puhl-kri-tyood'*) from the Latin, *pulchritudo*: beauty, from *pulcher, pulchr-*: beautiful

e.g. The rarely sighted offspring of Angelina Jolie and Brad Pitt will surely turn out to be models of **pulchritude**

purulent (adj.) = **unsightly (literally meaning, 'discharging pus')** (*pronounced 'pyoor-uh-luhnt'*) from the Latin, *purulentus*: festering, from *pus, pur-*: pus

e.g. Critics say Australia is no more than a collection of drive-ins, shopping arcades and **purulent** amusement parks

putative (adj.) = **reputed** *(pronounced 'pyoo-tuh-tiv')* from the Latin, *putat-*: thought, from *putare*: to think

e.g. In public, the politician claimed to have no party leadership aspirations; but privately he enjoyed the fact that he was the **putative** front-runner

(a) pyrrhic victory (set phrase) = **a victory won at too great a cost to have been worth it for the victor** *('pyrrhic' is pronounced 'pir-ik') for full explanation, see box below*

e.g. Killjoys said that London's winning of the mandate to host the 2012 Olympics was a **pyrrhic victory**, for the games cost billions of pounds at a time when the government could ill afford it

---

The phrase 'pyrrhic victory' derives from Pyrrhus (319–272 BC), a Greek general with a noted fondness for war elephants, who defeated the Roman army in a series of battles, but lost so many of his own troops in the process that it was hardly worth it.

In particular, when Pyrrhus invaded Apulia (in 279 BC) in 'the heel' of Italy, he sustained very heavy losses indeed – even though he won the battle overall. In total, Pyrrhus lost 3,500 men: almost as many as the Romans, who sustained 6,000 casualties. (In fact, so depleted were Pyrrhus's troops as a result, that Pyrrhus failed to capture the region's key city, Asculum, from the Romans.) It was this battle in Apulia that inspired the term 'pyrrhic victory', meaning a victory which comes at such a crippling cost that the victory is not in fact worth it.

Pyrrhus's death was particularly ignominious: in the course of a different battle – this time amidst the narrow streets of the Greek city of Argos – an old woman watching from a rooftop threw a tile onto Pyrrhus's head, stunning him. An enemy soldier then took his opportunity, and beheaded the discombobulated Pyrrhus.

Q

to put the quietus on (something) (set phrase) = **to finish off (something)** *('quietus' is pronounced 'kwahy-<u>ee</u>-tuhs')* from the Latin phrase, *quietus est*: he is quit; *the phrase was originally used as a form of verbal receipt on the payment of a debt*

e.g. The media were delighted when the politician refused to **put the quietus on** rumours that he would one day mount a leadership bid

quisling (noun) = **a traitor** *(pronounced '<u>kwiz</u>-ling') for full explanation, see box below*

e.g. The producers of every new reality TV show pray that one of their new recruits will turn into a vile **quisling**, as this will ensure a ratings boost

---

'quisling' derives from the name of Major Vidkun Quisling (1887–1945), a pastor's son who went on to become a politician, and then famously collaborated with the Nazis. It was in April 1940, following the German invasion of Norway, that Quisling seized power in a Nazi-backed coup d'état, ruling Norway on behalf of Hitler until 1945.

Quisling's collaborationist government took part – wittingly or unwittingly – in Germany's Final Solution. After World War II was over, Quisling was put on trial in Norway and found guilty of charges including murder and high treason. He was executed by firing squad in October 1945.

During World War II, the word 'quisling' became a synonym for 'traitor', and it has retained this sense ever since, no doubt helped by the wonderfully onomatopoeic sound of the surname 'Quisling', which suggests a kind of squelchy double-crossing.

---

quondam (adj.) = **erstwhile** *(pronounced '<u>kwon</u>-duhm')* from the Latin, *quondam*: former

e.g. Boris Johnson is the **quondam** editor of *The Spectator* magazine, which was allegedly known as *The Sextator* during his reign

rackety (adj.) = **making a loud noise, and therefore disreputable**
(*pronounced 'rak-i-tee'*) from the English words, *racket* + *-y*

e.g. The Chelsea Hotel in New York for many years epitomised its neighbourhood's **rackety** reputation

raddled (adj.) = *(of a person)* **old- or tired-looking** *from the English word 'ruddle' (which later evolved into the word 'raddle'), a red pigment used in make-up; an old- or tired-looking person needed more 'raddle' to enliven his appearance – and hence ended up well and truly 'raddled'*

e.g. After the birth of his first child and the ensuing sleeplessness, he began to look **raddled**

(a) rake's progress (set phrase) = **a gradual deterioration, owing to self-indulgence** *for full explanation, see box below*

e.g. Amy Winehouse's **rake's progress** began when she quit school early to join a jazz band

---

'A Rake's Progress' was the title given by 18th-century English artist William Hogarth to a series of eight paintings that he produced in 1732–33.

These eight paintings – which currently reside in the Soane Museum, London – depict the decline into destitution of Tom Rakewell, the son of a rich merchant, who comes to London, wastes all his money whoring and gambling, and as a consequence is imprisoned in the Fleet Prison and ultimately the lunatic asylum of Bedlam.

Over time, the term evolved to cover any example of debauched living that resulted in a downfall.

---

rapier-tongued (set phrase) = **having a very sharp tongue**
(*'rapier' is pronounced 'rey-pee-er'*) from *rapier*: a sword used for thrusting that is thin and sharp (and thus the kind of sword that most resembles a tongue) + *tongue*

e.g. In the film *Wall Street*, Michael Douglas played a **rapier-tongued** financier who famously says, 'Greed, for lack of a better word, is good'

reactionary

reactionary (noun) = **someone opposed to social liberalisation;** *literally, a 'reactionary' is 'someone who holds reactionary political views that mean they want a return to society's previous state (as a reaction against the current state)'* for full explanation, see box below

e.g. To his supporters, the Pope is a traditionalist; to his opponents, he is a **reactionary**

It was the French Revolution (1789–99) that gave us the word 'reactionary', which derives from the French word 'réactionnaire', denoting 'a movement advocating a return to a previous condition of affairs'.

The word 'réactionnaire' decribed those conservative forces – especially the Roman Catholic Church – that, believing national government to be the sole domain of the Church and of the state, opposed the social and economic changes brought by the revolution.

People who were 'réactionnaire' idealised the time before the French Revolution, when economies were mainly agrarian, society was ruled by a landed aristocracy headed by a hereditary king and the Roman Catholic Church was society's moral compass. Today the term 'reactionary' describes anyone wanting a return to more traditional values, who is opposed to 'progressive' liberal forces.

---

réclame (noun) = **public acclaim** (*pronounced 'rey-klahm'*) from the Old French, *réclamer*: to reclaim; from the Latin, *reclamare*: to cry out

e.g. The public sees politicians as being driven by a love of **réclame**, rather than by any desire to do good for society

recrudescence (noun) = **a fresh outbreak** (*pronounced 'ree-kroo-des-uhns'*) from the Latin, *recrudescere*: to become raw again, from *re-*: again + *crudus*: raw

e.g. When he bumped into his ex-wife in the frozen peas aisle of the supermarket, he experienced an unwelcome **recrudescence** of feeling

red in tooth and claw (set phrase) = *(of nature)* **merciless** *for full explanation, see box below*

e.g. Professor Richard Dawkins has said, '...the Darwinian world in which our ancestors were selected is a very unpleasant world. Nature really is **red in tooth and claw**...we should hold up Darwinism as an awful warning for how we should not organise our societies.'

The phrase 'red in tooth and claw' is a reference to the violent side of the natural world, and specifically to those moments – often featured on TV nature programmes – when predatory animals unsentimentally attack and devour their prey, turning their teeth and claws red (with blood) as a result.

It is from the poem 'In Memoriam A.H.H.' (1849) that the phrase comes; the poem's author was Lord Tennyson – formerly Poet Laureate of the United Kingdom . He penned the ode as a tribute to his best friend Arthur Hallam, also a poet and a fellow student at Cambridge, who was engaged to Tennyson's sister, but who died suddenly from a brain haemorrhage before the marriage could take place. This episode prompted Tennyson to write his poem, in order to express the conflict between a loving God and nature that was 'red in tooth and claw' (i.e. that had so cruelly snatched away his friend): a disparity that was a frequent concern of all Victorian thinkers. Here is the exact quote:

> *'Who trusted God was love indeed*
> *And love Creation's final law*
> *Tho' Nature, red in tooth and claw*
> *With ravine, shriek'd against his creed'*

(Incidentally, in the same poem, Tennyson also gave us the memorable lines: ''Tis better to have loved and lost, than never to have loved at all'.)

---

a red-letter day (set phrase) = **a day that is pleasantly memorable** *deriving from the medieval religious practice of printing holy days in the calendar in red ink*

e.g. Alfred Hitchcock looked back on his first occasion on set as a fully fledged director as **a red-letter day**

to redact (verb) = *(of a text)* **to edit for publication** *(pronounced 'ri-dakt')* from the Latin, *redact-,* the past participle stem of *redigere:* to reduce

e.g. Sometimes a judge will allow sensitive information in a case (involving national security, for example) to be **redacted**, before being released to the public

redoubtable (adj.) = *(of an opponent)* **formidable** *(pronounced 'ri-dou-tuh-buhl')* from the French, *redouter*: to fear, from *re-*: (expressing intensive force) + *douter*: to doubt

e.g. Osama bin Laden was, for many years, a **redoubtable** foe for the West

reductionist / reductive (adj.) = *(derogatory in tone)* **presenting a complex problem in a crudely simple way** *reductionist* is from the English words *reduction* + *-ist;* and *reductive* is from the Latin, *reducere*: to reduce

e.g. Journalist Charles Spencer has said of Lucian Freud's paintings, 'Living, breathing people are represented as little more than lumps of meat in a butcher's shop. It is a singularly **reductive** view of humanity.'

redux (adj. going after the noun) = **revived** *(pronounced 'ri-duhks')* from the Latin, *reducere*: to bring back

e.g. Critics say that *Golden Dawn* – the far-right political party that has gained a large share of the vote in Greece – is the Third Reich **redux**

refractory (adj.) = **stubborn, and impossible to manage** *(pronounced 'ri-frak-tuh-ree')* from the Latin, *refractarius:* stubborn, the past participle of *refringere*: to break up *(since, in science, a 'refractory material' means one that is hard to fuse together, and so, to manage)*

e.g. The little girl was thrown to the ground by the **refractory** pony

regnant (adj.) = **dominant** *(pronounced 'reg-nuhnt')* from the Latin, *regnant-*: reigning, from the verb, *regnare*: to rule

e.g. Amongst the liberal intelligentsia, the **regnant** view is that all Christians are deluded fools

to reify (something abstract) (verb) = **to make (something abstract) into a concrete thing** *(pronounced 'ree-uh-fahy')* from the Latin, *res, re-:* thing + *-fy*

e.g. For Hitchcock, his leading lady Grace Kelly was elegance **reified**

to rend your raiment over an event (set phrase) = **to tear your clothes (as a sign of extreme distress) over an event** *('raiment' is pronounced 'rey-muhnt')* from the English words, *to rend:* to tear into pieces + *raiment:* clothing *(a shortening of the now obsolete word, 'arrayment': 'dress')*

e.g. Fifty years ago, a divorce ruined your life; but nowadays most people don't **rend their raiment over** their marriage breaking up

to rescind (an agreement) (verb) = **to revoke (an agreement)** *(pronounced 'ri-sind')* from the Latin, *rescindere*, from *re-:* (expressing intensive force) + *scindere:* to divide

e.g. After he punched her in the face, she **rescinded** his invitation to her birthday party

to resile from (an agreement) (verb) = **to abandon (an agreement)** *('resile' is pronounced 'ri-zahyl')* from the French, *resilir*, from the Latin, *resilire:* to recoil, from *re-:* back + *salire:* to jump

e.g. Critics of Germany say the country must **resile from** its economic puritanism and allow more handouts to its neighbours in order to save the euro

restitution of (something) (noun) = **restoration of (something) to its orginal condition or owner** *(pronounced 'res-ti-too-shuhn')* from the Latin, *restituere:* to restore, from *re-:* again + *statuere:* to establish

e.g. Even if they privately support its return, most European political leaders are too politically savvy to call for the **restitution of** the death penalty

restive

---

restive (adj.) = **restless** from the French, *restif, -ive*, from *rester*: to remain, ultimately from the Latin, *restare*: to remain; *the original sense was 'to remain still', but then the connotation of 'unmanageable' evolved via the notion of a horse remaining still in defiance, refusing to move forward*

e.g. Her friend had warned her about the seven-year itch, and, sure enough, shortly after she'd celebrated her seventh wedding anniversary, she grew **restive**

revenant (noun) = **a person who has returned, often supposedly from the dead** *(pronounced 'rev-uh-nuhnt')* from the French, *revenant*: coming back, the present participle of *revenir*: to come back

e.g. I returned to the city where I was born, but no one recognised me there, so I walked around unnoticed, a lonely **revenant**

revisionist (adj.) = *(of a person)* **revising one's opinions about a previously accepted point of view (with the implication of 'selling out')** *for full explanation, see box below*

e.g. If a Hollywood film were to cast Jesus as the villain and Pilate as the hero, religious groups would object to such a **revisionist** take on the Bible

---

The phrase 'revisionist' is a pejorative term originally used in the 19th century by supporters of Karl Marx, to describe socialist writers such as Eduard Bernstein. Marx's supporters were irked by Bernstein because he sought to revise Marx's ideas about the means of transition to socialism, claiming that a socialist society could be achieved through peaceful and gradual methods rather than by Marx's chosen method of a violent revolution. 'Revisionist', therefore, was a term used of Bernstein to imply he was a traitor to the Marxist cause.

In the 1940s and 1950s, the term cropped up again; this time it was used by Stalinists who affixed the 'revisionist' label to those communists who advocated the production of consumer goods (rather than of heavy industry), and who encouraged democratic, non-communist reforms (instead of promoting a communist revolution).

Since then, 'revisionism' has been a charge levelled by one group at any other group who is seen as going against a premise originally shared by both groups.

to roister (verb) = **to enjoy oneself in a noisy manner**
(*pronounced 'roi-ster'*) from the French, *rustre*: ruffian, variant of
ruste, from *rusticus*: rustic

e.g. After the stockmarket shuts at 4.30 p.m., traders gather in
the City's bars to **roister**

roman à clef (set phrase) = **a novel in which real people and
situations appear but with made up names** (*pronounced
'raw-mah na kley'*) from the French, *roman à clef*: novel with a key
(*the key being the one that unlocks the relationship between the
non-fictional and the fictional worlds, between the real people depicted
and the characters in the novel; this key is often implied by the author
via literary devices within the novel*)

e.g. Ernest Hemingway's *The Sun Also Rises* (1926) – a barely
disguised account of Hemingway's life as a writer in Paris, and his
1925 voyage to Spain with several known personalities – is a
classic **roman à clef**

Rorschach test (noun) = ***(in psychology)* a test in which a
person is presented with various ink blots on paper, and asked
what shapes he or she sees in them (the answers reflect what is
on the person's mind)** (*'Rorschach' is pronounced 'roar-shak'*)
*deriving from the name of the test's creator, Hermann Rorschach
(1884–1922), a Swiss psychiatrist*

e.g. She pointed out a cloud above us; to me, it
looked like a soft meringue, but she said she
saw a menacing shark in it. This unwittingly
undertaken **Rorschach test** was the first sign to
me of her fearful personality

roseate (adj.) = **optimistic; *'roseate' literally
means 'rose-coloured' (and hence 'optimistic', as
per the expression 'rose-tinted glasses')***
(*pronounced 'roh-zee-it'*) from the Latin, *roseus*:
rosy, from *rosa*: rose + -*ate*

e.g. Pessimists say there is a gulf between the
roseate ideals of marriage and its prosaic
day-to-day reality

(to be) the Rosetta Stone of (a field of knowledge)

(to be) the Rosetta Stone of (a field of knowledge)
(set phrase) = **to be the essential key to (a new field of knowledge)** *for full explanation, see box below*

e.g. Scientists are desperate to find the 'missing-link' fossil that links man to ape (known as the 'hominoid gap'), which would be the **Rosetta Stone of** evolution

---

The 'Rosetta Stone' refers to an actual stone bearing this name, the most visited object in the British Museum in London. Inscribed on this stone – discovered in 1799 in Rosetta, a place in Egypt near the Nile – is a decree issued by King Ptolemy V of Egypt in 196 BC.

Significantly, this same decree from the king was written out fully both in Ancient Greek and in Egyptian hieroglyphs. Before the discovery of the 'Rosetta Stone', no one had been able to make sense of Egyptian hieroglyphs – but Ancient Greek had never been a problem. So, for the first time, academics could suddenly understand Egyptian hieroglyphs (since they could make sense of the corresponding Greek text – which contained exactly the same meaning as that in the hieroglyphs – as a key).

And suddenly they could also understand all the other early records of Ancient Egyptian civilisation and literature (that had also been written out in hieroglyphs) – such as 'The Pyramid Texts', which were reserved only for the Pharaoh's eyes, and which contained spells for allowing him to fly and for reanimating his body after death. Today the term 'Rosetta Stone' is used to refer to an essential clue that illuminates a whole field of knowledge.

to cross the Rubicon (set phrase) = **to go past the point of no return** *for full explanation, see box below*

e.g. When Japanese planes attacked Pearl Harbour in 1941, US President Franklin D. Roosevelt decided **to cross the Rubicon** and become fully involved in World War II

The phrase 'to cross the Rubicon' refers to an important river in Italy, the Rubicon, which, during the Roman Republic (509–27 BC), was the designated boundary separating Italy proper (controlled by Rome and the Senate) from the Roman province of Cisalpine Gaul (equivalent to the northernmost part of modern-day Italy).

When Julius Caesar – fresh from his conquest of the whole of Gaul – boldly crossed this Rubicon river and entered Italy with his army in 49 BC, he went past the point of no return: this crossing was a clear sign that he had declared war on Rome, for Roman generals (such as Caesar) were strictly forbidden by Rome to lead an army into Italy proper.

After three years of bloody fighting, Caesar ended up winning the ensuing civil war within the Roman Republic, which led eventually to the establishment of the Roman Empire (27 BC–AD 476) by Caesar's adopted heir Octavius (rather than by Caesar himself, who was assassinated by Brutus five years after his crossing of the Rubicon).

rubicund (adj.) = **red-faced** *(pronounced 'roo-bi-kuhnd')* from the Latin, *rubicundus*, from *rubere*: to be red

e.g. In film adaptations of *Sherlock Holmes*, Dr Watson is traditionally portrayed as a good-natured, **rubicund** companion to the great detective

rubric (noun) = **a guideline** *(pronounced 'roo-brik')* from the Latin, *rubrica*: red; *originally, 'rubric' referred in religious books to rules regarding conduct during a religious ceremony – these rules were written out in red, to make them stand out from the prayers making up the rest of the book*

e.g. Although it seems to make little difference to the country's finances, politicians periodically unveil a new **rubric** for economic growth

---

ruminative (adj.) = **thinking deeply about a topic** *(pronounced 'roo-muh-nit-iv')* from the Latin, *ruminat-* : chewed over, from *ruminari*: to chew over (like a cow)

e.g. When news broke of JFK's assassination, most people fell into a **ruminative** silence

runnel (noun) = **a small stream** from the Middle English, *rynel*: a small stream, ultimately from the Old English, *rinnan*: to run

e.g. As he cocked his gun and pushed open the door to the bank, he felt a **runnel** of sweat coursing down his back

sagacious (adj.) = **shrewd** (*pronounced 'suh-gey-shuhs'*) from the Latin, *sagax, sagac-:* wise + *-ious*

e.g. With a self-made fortune of tens of billions of dollars, Warren Buffett has a reputation as one the most **sagacious** investors alive

salad days (pl. noun) = **a time of youthful inexperience and indiscretion** *for full explanation, see box below*

e.g. On a rainy day, Elizabeth Taylor no doubt enjoyed flicking through the photos of her eight marriages and casting her mind back to the **salad days** of each relationship

---

'salad days' was a phrase coined by Shakespeare in his play Antony and Cleopatra *(1606); at one point, Cleopatra, regretting her youthful dalliances with Julius Caesar, says, '...My salad days, / When I was green in judgement, cold in blood...'*

Shakespeare chose the image of the salad because the qualities Cleopatra associates with this youthful time are 'green in judgement' *and* 'cold in blood': *two adjectives that may equally well be used of a nice, crunchy salad. Almost straight away, the phrase 'salad days' entered the mainstream, as shorthand to describe an immature phase in one's life.*

The term has featured in many films and songs; for example, the band Spandau Ballet *(who were massive in the 1980s) referenced the expression in their song 'Gold', when they extended Cleopatra's metaphor thus: 'These are my salad days, slowly being eaten away.'*

samizdat

samizdat (noun) = **books that had to be secretly published and distributed, because they'd been banned by the state (especially in the former USSR)** (*pronounced 'sah-miz-daht'*) *for full explanation, see box below*

e.g. The only practical information that the pupils ever got about sex was a **samizdat** sheet of illustrations circulated by one 'progressive' teacher

---

'samizdat' is a Russian word, meaning 'a self-publishing house'. Between 1953 (when Stalin died) and 1988 (when Mikhail Gorbachev gave new freedoms to the Russian people, via the process of 'glasnost'), the word 'samizdat' was used by Russians to describe books banned by the state (usually because these books offered political or religious views opposed to the state). To avoid detection, these forbidden tomes had to be painstakingly written out by hand, then passed carefully from reader to reader. Harsh punishments were doled out to those caught with a 'samizdat' edition.

An example of such a banned book is Dr Zhivago (1957). Despite containing no overt messages of political dissent, the book was outlawed because it apparently focused excessively on the views of individual characters, rather than on the welfare of the state. (The book enjoyed huge popularity in its 'samizdat' form.)

One intriguing aspect of 'samizdat' is that many of its readers were in fact Russian state officials – for, to work out if a book should be banned, it had first to be read by these apparatchiks. (And 'samizdat' copies of books have, of course, appeared outside Russia, too, in other countries where the state has sought to exercise total control: in Iran, for example, Salman Rushdie's 1988 book The Satanic Verses, emerged in 'samizdat' form after it had been officially banned.)

---

sans serif (adj.) = **(*describing a style of font*) aggressively plain, i.e. devoid of that final flourish of a tiny ornate line at the top or bottom of each letter** (*pronounced 'son ser-if'*) from the French, *sans*: without + *serif*: a tiny ornate line (as above), from the Dutch, *schreef*: a line

e.g. To give a down-to-earth impression to its customers, most Internet companies go in for modish **sans serif** logos

sapient (adj.) = wise; OR *(derogatory in tone)* apparently wise **(but not in fact so)** *(pronounced 'sey-pee-uhnt')* from the Latin, *sapient-*: being wise

e.g. Many people believe that planets other than our own also contain **sapient** life

sapphic (adj.) = *(formal in tone)* lesbian *(pronounced 'saf-ik')* for full explanation, see box below

e.g. The film *The Kids are All Right* (2010) – which charts the lives of a married lesbian couple based in California – is a tale of **sapphic** love

---

'sapphic' derives from 'Sappho', the name of an Ancient Greek poetess who lived on the isle of Lesbos (which also gives us the word 'lesbian') in c. 600 BC. The 3rd-century philosopher Maximus of Tyre wrote that Sappho was a 'small and dark' woman.

Sappho was also a great poet, so esteemed in the ancient world that she was deemed to be Homer's equal. Until Sappho came along, poetry had been used almost exclusively to sing the praises of dead soldiers, but Sappho had the temerity to use the first person in her poetry (a bold innovation for the time) and to discuss complex human emotions, particularly the erotic. Modern literary critics have praised the startling imagery in Sappho's work: 'Love shook my heart like a wind falling on the oaks of a mountain', is one of her lines. Sappho was married and had a daughter, yet she wrote love poems addressed to both men and women (though her poems contain zero physical descriptions of lesbian encounters).

The English word 'sapphic' wasn't invented, though, until Victorian times, when French novelist Pierre Louys (1870–1925) claimed to have come across the poems of an ancient Lesbian poetess named Bilitis, who allegedly lived around Sappho's time. The Bilitis poems were teeming with salacious details and lesbian sex galore; in time, the poet Bilitis – who was apparently a contemporary of Sappho – became confused with the poet Sappho in popular culture, and so everyone assumed Sappho's work was full of lesbian sex, too. (This false impression survived intact even when the Bilitis poems were later revealed to be a hoax, perpetrated by this prurient Frenchman, Pierre Louys, who claimed to have 'discovered' them.) Today, then, the adjective 'sapphic' exclusively conjures up images of lesbian sex (which never actually appeared in the poet Sappho's work).

saturnalia

saturnalia (noun) = **a wild party** *(pronounced 'sat-er-ney-lee-uh')*
for full explanation, see box below

e.g. Various writers have produced new Bond stories recently, featuring Fleming's original **saturnalia** of daring deeds, beautiful women and cruel villains

---

'saturnalia' means in Latin: 'matters relating to the god Saturn', and refers to the ancient Roman festival of Saturn held in late December, a period of general merrymaking.

In Roman mythology, Saturn was an agricultural deity who reigned over the world in the 'Golden Age': a time of peace, referred to in Greek mythology, when humans enjoyed the bounty of the earth, without needing to work, and a state of complete social equality. Reflecting these beliefs, the 'saturnalia' holiday was celebrated with a sacrifice at the Temple of Saturn in the Roman Forum, followed by a large public banquet and a carnival that overturned Roman social norms: gambling was allowed, and masters provided table service for their slaves, who were also permitted to insult their masters. The poet Catullus called it 'the best of days'.

The celebrations of the 'saturnalia' continued into the 4th century AD; and, as the Roman Empire came under Christian rule, some of the tamer customs from the 'saturnalia' – including its timing, in late December – proceeded to inform the seasonal celebrations behind our own Christmas and New Year celebrations.

---

satyr (noun) = **a man who is highly sexed** *(pronounced 'sat-er') in Greek and Roman myth, a 'satyr' was a lecherous and drunken woodland god; theirs was a strong look, being half-man and half-goat (with a man's body but a goat's ears, tail, legs and horns)*

e.g. In his naked self-portrait *Painter Working* (1993), Lucian Freud painted himself as an ageing **satyr**

(the) old saw (set phrase) = **the old saying** from the Old English, *sagu*: a saying, related to the German, *sage:* legend

e.g. 'Give me the boy until he is seven and I will show you the man', runs the **old saw,** allegedly coined by the Jesuit religious order

schlock (noun) = **inferior goods, trash** (*pronounced 'shlok'*) from the Yiddish, *shlak,* ultimately from the German, *Schlacke*: scum, dross

e.g. Critics of Walt Disney say he survived only by peddling his **schlock** to the most uncritical of audiences: children

screed (noun) = **a long and tedious piece of writing** (*pronounced 'skreed'*) *'screed' started out as a variant of the noun 'shred'; so, the meaning was originally 'a shredded fragment, torn from a speech', then evolved to mean 'a long torn strip of words', and, in time, 'a long roll of writing'*

e.g. Many of the academics who publicly hail James Joyce's *Ulysses* as the greatet novel ever written, in private dismiss the 1,000-page book as a **screed**

to scry in (one's mirror or crystal ball) (verb) = **to foretell the future (using one's mirror or crystal ball)** from a shortening (in 1520) of the English, *to descry:* to catch sight of

e.g. George Soros is such a prescient investor, that it is as if he **scrys in his mirror** before making a purchase

scuttlebutt (noun) = *(informal in tone)* **gossip** *a 'scuttlebutt' originally meant, in 1805, a 'water cask kept on a ship's deck'; then, since sailors used to gather around this scuttlebutt / water cask for a good gossip, in time 'scuttlebutt' evolved to mean 'gossip'*

e.g. Journalists are skilled at transforming mere **scuttlebutt** into plausible-sounding reports – often by inserting statements like 'a close friend said...'

to secede from (a union) (verb) = **to withdraw formally from (a union)** (*pronounced 'si-seed'*) from the Latin, *secedere,* from *se-*: apart + *cedere*: to go

e.g. It was not until 1830 that Belgium **seceded from** the Netherlands

seer (noun) = *(humorous in tone)* **an expert who provides forecasts of the future in a particular field, such as economics or sport** from the English words, *see + -er; a 'seer' originally referred, in the 14th century, to a person who was supposed to be able to predict the future owing to a supernatural insight*

e.g. When England was knocked out of the Euro 2012 football championships, the **seers** on the BBC sofa looked stunned

to semaphore (a message) (verb) = **to send (a message) as if by semaphore** *(a visual signalling apparatus with mechanically moving arms, used on train tracks)* (pronounced '<u>sem</u>-uh-fohr') for full explanation, see box below

e.g. Over dinner, she sat turned towards him, her legs pointing in his direction and her entire body **semaphoring** her desire

'to semaphore' comes from the French, 'semaphore': 'a bearer of signals', and ultimately from the Greek, 'sema': 'signal' + 'phoros': 'bearer', from 'pherein': 'to carry'.

A 'semaphore' was one of the earliest forms of fixed railway signal; it consisted of an erect pole, placed right next to a railway track. Out of this jutted an 'arm' (often made of metal) that, via its particular angle of inclination, provided a variety of indications to approaching train drivers.

After the design was patented in the early 1840s, the 'semaphore' soon became the most widely used form of mechanical signal in the world. Nowadays, though, colour light signals have replaced semaphore signals in many countries. But the term 'to semaphore a message' is still used to convey the sense of someone desperately signalling a communication – such as romantic interest – to someone else.

serried (adj.) = *(of rows of people or things)* **tightly packed together** (pronounced '<u>ser</u>-eed') from the French, *serré*: close together, ultimately based on the Latin, *sera*: lock

e.g. During the protests against capitalism in London, **serried** ranks of tents could be seen outside St Paul's Cathedral

sesquipedalian (adj.) = *(of a person)* **using long words** (pronounced 'ses-kwi-pi-<u>dey</u>-lee-uhn') for full explanation, see box opposite

e.g. Many academics are difficult to understand because they're **sesquipedalian**

'sesquipedalian' finds its origins in Roman times, when the poet Horace wrote a work called Ars Poetica (The Art of Poetry) *in 18 BC.*

In it, Horace criticised overlong words and used a purposefully long expression to define such words: 'sesquipedalia verba', meaning literally 'words that are a foot and a half long' (from the Latin, 'sesqui-': 'half as much again' + 'pes': 'foot', thus evoking the image of a word that is 50 per cent longer than a standard one).

---

shamanic (adj.) = **spiritual, but unhinged** *(pronounced 'shey-muhn-ik') for full explanation, see box below*

e.g. In the *Pirates of the Carribbean* film series, Johnny Depp's character Captain Jack Sparrow, with his blackened eyes and flowing robes, emits a decidedly **shamanic** air

---

The word 'shaman' – originally a Russian word that is ultimately from the Sanskrit 'srama', meaning 'a religious exercise' – came to the West in 1692, after first evolving in Russia, Mongolia and China.

A 'shaman' was a man prized within a tribe for his magical powers – specifically for his ability to enter the spirit world, and come back with solutions for any health problems afflicting the living. This gift apparently derived from the fact that he had himself once been gravely ill (but had then recovered), allowing him a brief insight into the other world and into cures for illnesses. In order to enter their spiritual trance (necessary for the curing process), shamans used a variety of catalysts, notably drugs (such as cannabis and cactus plants), music (especially drums) and even activities such as sword-fighting.

Shamans used to be prevalent across most cultures, but now only exist in a few places, such as Africa and Papua New Guinea. The adjective 'shamanic' today is used to evoke the image of someone slightly unhinged (perhaps in a nod to every shaman's necessary brush with death, as described earlier) but with a peculiar insight into spiritual matters. Captain Jack Sparrow, the character played by Johnny Depp in Pirates of the Caribbean: At World's End, *for example, is of this type, in the sense that he is tinged with madness (after extended solitary confinement in Davy Jones's Locker), and now desires communion with the spirit world (as evidenced by his quest for immortality).*

Shavian

Shavian (adj.) = *(of drama)* strongly promoting a social message, but also witty *(like the plays of George Bernard Shaw)* for *full explanation, see box below*

e.g. Critics described the new play – which depicted the squalid living conditions of some immigrants in the United Kingdom, but also burst with witticisms – as a **Shavian** masterpiece

---

'Shavian' is from 'Shavius', a Latinised version of the surname 'Shaw' – specifically, George Bernard Shaw (1856–1950), the Irish playwright who revolutionised London theatre and who was, by the end of his life, famed throughout the world. Shaw was a strong socialist who was particularly keen – like Charles Dickens before him – to highlight the exploitation of the working classes. In his plays, this social commentary was leavened by healthy dollops of humourous quotes in the style of his contemporary, Oscar Wilde (1854–1900).

Shaw's most famous play is Pygmalion *(1912), which was later transformed into the more famous musical film* My Fair Lady *(1964), starring Audrey Hepburn and Rex Harrison. In Greek mythology, Pygmalion was a man who created a statue of a woman out of ivory; later the statue comes to life. Shaw explored this same theme in his play, which centres around Henry Higgins, a professor of phonetics, and his training up of cockney flower girl Eliza Doolittle, with the goal of passing her off as a duchess at an ambassador's garden party. Shaw's social message was clear: as well as highlighting the suppression of women at that time, the play is a satire of the British class system. And humourous quotes – that other hallmark of 'Shavian' drama – enliven the action, such as this observation by Eliza's father: 'I have to live for others and not for myself: that's middle class morality.'*

Shaw led a long and varied life, and also co-founded the LSE (London School of Economics) amongst other achievements. He was noted, too, for his unusual marriage, which was never consummated – at his wife's insistence.

---

shtick (noun) = **an entertainment routine (to get attention)**
(pronounced 'shtik') from the Yiddish, *shtik*: an act, ultimately from the German, *stück*: play

e.g. Leslie Nielsen's bumbling straight-man **schtick** made him one of Hollywood's leading comedy acts in films such as *The Naked Gun 2 ½: The Smell of Fear*

sibylline (adj.) = *(of a person)* giving out enigmatic-sounding predictions about the future *(like a Sibyl, a Greek oracle)* (pronounced '<u>sib</u>-uh-line') *for full explanation, see box below*

e.g. The French pharmacist Nostradamus (1503–66) is still famed for his **sibylline** statements such as, 'After there is great trouble among mankind, a greater one is prepared'

The word 'sibylline' comes from the Greek word, 'sibylla', meaning 'prophetess'. There were many sibyls in the ancient world; the earliest ones issued their prophecies at certain holy sites, and were said to be under divine influence. Sibyls did not have a name of their own, but were known by a place name referring to the location of their holy site.

For example, the Erythraean Sibyl was famous in around the 7th century BC for her prophesising under the divine influence of the god at Erythrae (a town in Ionia, now Turkey). This particular Sibyl is supposed to have predicted the Trojan War, but in a very mysterious way - by writing on leaves, then arranging these leaves so that the initial letters of each leaf also formed a word. (Hence 'sibylline' still refers today to a prediction about the future, one delivered in an enigmatic way.)

Michelangelo (1475-1564) provided us with the most iconic vision of the sibyls, which can still be seen in the frescos of the Sistine Chapel in Rome; in the painter's depiction, they are female but so aged that it's hard to tell their sex.

---

signally *(adv.)* = **notably** from the French, *signalé:* distinguished, the past participle of *signaller*

e.g. For years, the world **signally** failed to stop Hitler murdering so many Jews

simian (adj.) = **like a monkey** *(pronounced '<u>sim</u>-ee-uhn')* from the Latin, *simia*: ape, from the Greek, *simos*: flat-nosed

e.g. People with a **simian** appearance are often considered attractive, as their features are usually quite neat

sinecure (noun) = **a position requiring very little work, but which does pay a salary** (*pronounced 'sahy-ni-kyoor'*) from the Latin, *sine cura*: without care

e.g. Most non-executive directorships are really **sinecures**, paying £20,000 a year for perhaps five days' work per month

Sino- *(+ another country)* (combining form) = **Chinese and** *(another country)* from the Latin, *Sinae*: the Chinese, ultimately from the Arabic, *Sin*: China

e.g. Aware that China will be the biggest economy in the world by 2020, American politicians are united in their desire to forge a stronger **Sino-**American relationship

Sisyphean (adj.) = *(of a task)* **pointless and endless** (*pronounced 'sis-if-ee-uhn'*) for full explanation, see box below

e.g. Holding together a coalition government – made up of constantly diverging views – must be a **Sisyphean** task

---

'Sisyphean' is from the Greek name 'Sisuphos' ('Sisyphus'), a man who severely offended the gods, and, as punishment, was condemned to the eternal task of rolling a large boulder to the top of a hill, from which it always rolled down again.

Sisyphus was the first king of Ephyra (later the Greek city of Corinth); and, from Homer onwards, Sisyphus was famed as the craftiest of men. At the end of his life, when Thanatos, king of the dead, came to claim him, Sisyphus' cunning came to the fore; he slyly asked Thanatos to demonstrate how the chains (intended for Sisyphus) actually worked. With Thanatos all thrust up as a result of his ensuing demonstration, Sisyphus scarpered. This caused an uproar since no human on earth could die with Thanatos thus incapacitated. (Eventually the god of war, Ares – who was particularly irked by this turn of events, since Ares' battles had suddenly lost their sparkle now that no one could actually die any more – freed Thanatos from his chains.)

As punishment for this and other acts of trickery, Zeus, king of the gods, made Sisyphus roll a huge stone up a steep hill for all eternity: when Sisyphus had pushed the stone to the top, it always rolled back down, forcing him to begin the task again, in an endless loop. Zeus purposefully chose this devilish punishment to prove to Sisyphus that he, Sisyphus, was not as clever as Zeus – despite Sisyphus' hubristic belief to the contrary. And pointless and interminable activities are still described as 'Sisyphean' today.

skein (noun) = **a tangled arrangement** (*pronounced 'skayn'*) from the Middle English *skeine*, ultimately from the Old French, *escaigne*: a coil of yarn

e.g. She had plastic surgery to remove the **skeins** of crows' feet clustered around her eyes

slattern (noun) = **a dirty, untidy woman** (*pronounced 'slat-ern'*) from the Old English verb, *to slatter*: to splash awkwardly (*historically used of women considered untidy*)

e.g. Every morning on the way to work, I see a **slattern** pushing a supermarket trolley on the other side of the road

snaggletoothed (adj.) = **having bad teeth (that are either broken or jutting out)** from the English word, *snaggletooth*: a deep-sea fish with unappealing-looking teeth

e.g. It's virtually impossible for a **snaggletoothed** actor to make it in Hollywood

to cock a snook at (someone / something) (set phrase) = **to show contempt for (someone / something)** *'to cock a snook at' literally means 'to place one's hand so that the thumb touches one's nose and the fingers are spread out, so as to show contempt' (of unknown origin)*

e.g. During his lifetime, Kim Jong Il never missed an opportunity to **cock a snook at** the United States

sodality (noun) = **an association (often religious)** (*pronounced 'soh-dal-i-tee'*) from the Latin, *sodalitas*: sodality, from *sodalis*: comrade

e.g. In Dan Brown's novel *The Da Vinci Code*, some of the villains are members of Opus Dei, a **sodality** of Catholics

(a) solvent of *(a negative situation)* (set phrase) = **something that acts to solve** *(a negative situation)* (*pronounced 'sol-vuhnt'*) from the Latin, *solvent-*: loosening, from *solvere*: to loosen; *the precise way in which a 'solvent' solves a negative situation is by dissolving (or loosening) it*

e.g. A hug from a friend is **a solvent of** loneliness

somatic (adj.) = **relating to the body (as opposed to the mind)** (*pronounced 'soh-mat-ik'*) from the Greek, *somatikos*: of the body, from *soma*: body

e.g. You feel powerful emotions not just in your head but also **somatically**, in your gut

to sough (verb) = *(of the wind or of the sea)* **to make a moaning sound** (*pronounced 'suf'*) from the Old English, *swogan*: to make a moaning sound

e.g. The only sound was the wind **soughing**

sphinx (noun) = **an inscrutable person, who keeps their thoughts secret** *for full explanation, see box below*

e.g. The enigmatic François Mitterand was long regarded as the **sphinx** of French politics

---

The word 'sphinx' comes from the Greek word 'sphinx', used of a winged monster from Greek mythology, with the head of a woman and the body of a lioness. (The Greek word 'sphinx' itself ultimately derives from the Greek 'sphingein', meaning 'to squeeze' – perhaps because lionesses kill their prey by squeezing and strangling them until the breath leaves them. The word 'sphincter'– which likewise does a lot of squeezing – derives from the same Greek root.)

The sphinx of Greek mythology is said to have guarded the entrance to the ancient Greek city of Thebes, and to have posed to any traveller wanting to enter the city, the most famous riddle in history: 'Which creature walks on four legs in the morning, two legs in the afternoon and three legs in the evening?' Anyone unable to answer this question, the sphinx would strangle, then devour. In the end, it was Oedipus who solved the riddle, answering, 'Man, who crawls on all fours as a baby, then walks on two feet as an adult, and then with a cane (i.e. three 'feet') in old age.' The sphinx's response to her riddle being cracked thus was to commit suicide by hurling herself from the high rock on which she sat.

To this day, you can see huge stone sphinxes next to the Pyramids in Egypt, with their human faces and lions' bodies. And the word 'sphinx' is still used to refer to anyone whose inscrutable appearance calls to mind the sphinx of ancient Greek mythology, who steadfastly refused to reveal the answer to her riddle.

spiel (noun) = **plausible but glib talk** *(often employed by salespeople)* *(pronounced 'shpeel')* from the German, *spiel*: a game

e.g. When he spotted in his forecourt the young couple with their matching Rolex watches, the car salesman rubbed his hands, sidled over and began his **spiel**

spoliation (noun) = **the act of plundering** *(pronounced 'spoh-lee-ey-shuhn')* from the Latin, *spoliare*: to strip skin from an animal

e.g. The London riots were characterised by looting and **spoliation**

spoor (noun) = **the trail left by a human or by an animal** *(pronounced 'spore')* from the Old English, *spor*: footprint

e.g. He held her wineglass up to the light: her lipstick stain was still there, and he spent a few minutes marvelling at this, her **spoor**

Stakhanovite

Stakhanovite (noun) = **an exceptionally industrious worker**
(pronounced 'stuh-<u>kan</u>-uh-vite') *for full explanation, see box below*

e.g. The creator of *Peanuts*, Charles M. Schulz, took only one
vacation – lasting just five weeks – during the whole 50 years the
cartoon ran for: his was a **Stakhanovite** work ethic

*The word 'Stakhanovite' derives from the name of Soviet coal
miner Aleksei Grigorevich Stakhanov (1906–77), an exceptionally
hard worker whose feats of productivity were held up by the
Soviet government as a prime example of the efficiency of the
socialist economic system.*

*Born in Russia, Stakhanov began working in a mine in the Ukraine
in 1927. His strength and skills apparently changed overnight in
1935, when he took a local course in mining: soon afterwards, it
was reported by the Soviet authorities that he'd mined 14 times as
much coal as his quota required (to be precise, a record 102
tonnes of coal in under six hours). In the resulting blaze of
publicity, his face was splashed across newspapers and posters,
and his craggy features even attracted the attention of the world
at large, when he graced the cover of* Time *magazine. In the
Soviet Union, he was held up as a model of worker productivity for
the whole country to emulate: Stalin parlayed Stakhanov's records
into the Stakhanovite movement, where workers who exceeded
production targets were rewarded with the title 'Stakhanovite'
(and anyone opposing the movement was labelled a 'wrecker').*

*Scorn has since been poured on the validity of Stakhanov's record.
In 1985,* The New York Times *printed a story alleging that
Stakhanov was in fact secretly aided by many other workers to
break the record (so as to boost Communist party morale).
Regardless, it's still Aleksei Grigorevich Stakhanov's name – and
his alone – that is evoked today when we describe
someone very industrious as 'Stakhanovite'.*

statist (adj.) = *(of a political system)* **with the state in exclusive control of the economy** *(pronounced 'stey-tist')* from the English words, *state* + *ist*

e.g. After the credit crunch, people are less keen on capitalism and are now more accepting of **statist** policies by governments

statuary (noun) = **statues, regarded as a collective**
(pronounced 'statue-ary') from the Latin, *statua*: stood up, from *stare*: to stand

e.g. In films about the Roman empire, the villas of the rich are full of slaves and **statuary**

stalking horse

stalking horse (set phrase) = *(usually in politics)* a minor player who challenges the party leader (so that the minor player's patron, a more powerful figure in the shadows, can gauge – before announcing his own candidature – whether there is any demand for a new leader) *for full explanation, see box below*

e.g. When the largely unknown back-bench politician Sir Anthony Meyer challenged Margaret Thatcher in 1989 for the Conservative Party leadership, journalists speculated that Sir Anthony was a **stalking horse** for a more credible candidate

The term 'stalking horse' started life in the 16th century, originally deriving from the practice of hunting wild ducks. Hunters noticed that these ducks – which would fly off immediately if approached by humans – would happily tolerate the close presence of horses. Availing themselves of this knowledge, the human hunters – all crouched down and keeping their upper bodies hidden – would walk alongside their horses and, in this way, be able to gradually approach the ducks (who apparently did not notice that they were being approached by a six-legged horse) until the ducks were within firing range. Horses used for this purpose were called 'stalking horses'.

In a similar way, in politics, a 'stalking horse' is an individual who provides cover for another, more powerful person to attack. Specifically, in politics, a 'stalking horse' throws his hat into the ring, to see if there's any demand for a change of party leader. The 'stalking horse' will be a minor figure, with a pretty much zero chance of being accepted as leader himself; but his leadership challenge will have 'tested the water' for a far more powerful player watching from the shadows. (Likewise, in business, a minor company might make a 'stalking horse' bid for another company, to see how the bid target reacts to the price proposed; then a more powerful company – who now knows what the lowest acceptable price is – will come in and finish off the target.) In both cases, the minor figure of the 'stalking horse' and the major player behind the scenes are in cahoots all along; the incentive for the 'stalking horse' is that he will gain the patronage of the more powerful figure.

In the case of Sir Anthony Meyer, he launched his leadership bid against Margaret Thatcher when support for her was waning, shortly after Nigel Lawson resigned as Chancellor. (So minor a figure was Sir Anthony that the press went so far as to label him 'a stalking donkey'.) But the resulting leadership election did show that many MPs had lost confidence in Margaret Thatcher, and in the end, she was replaced by John Major, in 1990. (In this particular case, Sir Anthony seems not to have been in cahoots with any other MP in particular, but just wished to act as a catalyst to plunge Maggie into a leadership battle with others more powerful than himself. Later, Sir Anthony Meyer was deselected by his constituency party for his 'treachery' towards Margaret Thatcher, and a tabloid paper revealed he'd conducted a decades-long extra-marital affair with a former model and blues singer.)

to stonewall (a question) (verb) = **to refuse to answer (a question)** *for full explanation, see box below*

e.g. When he confronted his wife with the hotel room receipt as evidence of her adultery, she **stonewalled** his questions and stormed out of the house

The term 'stonewall' first appeared as a nickname for General Thomas J. Jackson (1824–63), to describe his unyielding stance in war. General Jackson fought in the American Civil War (1861–5); he was on the side of the Confederate States, the name for the 11 Southern states who severed their links with the rest of the United States (following Abraham Lincoln's 1860 election victory and subsequent avowal to phase out slavery: anathema to the highly profitable cotton states of the Deep South, who relied heavily on slave labour).

Jackson earned his famous nickname 'stonewall' in 1861, owing to his behaviour in one particular battle. As Jackson's side began to crumble under a heavy enemy assault, Jackson's brigade provided crucial reinforcements, and the sight of Jackson refusing to yield led to a fellow commander allegedly shouting, 'There is Jackson standing like a stone wall. Let us determine to die here, and we will conquer.'

He may have been on the losing side in the war, but Jackson's nickname of 'stonewall' is still used today, to evoke a similarly non-yielding position in the face of a verbal (rather than a physical) assault.

stool pigeon (noun) = an informer (especially for the police)
'stool pigeon' alludes to the 19th-century practice of tying a pigeon to a stool in order to attract other pigeons, which were then shot

e.g. When the drug-running gang discovered he was a **stool pigeon**, they killed him

stratified (adj.) = *(of a group)* arranged into different layers or **strata** *(pronounced 'strat-uh-fahyd')* from the Latin, *stratum*: horizontal layer

e.g. The United Kingdom is more obsessed with class structure than the United States and, as a result, the United Kingdom is more socially **stratified**

to attack a straw man (set phrase) = *(in politics)* to give the false impression of having refuted an opponent's argument when you've, in fact, merely replaced the real argument with a superficially similar (but weaker) proposition that is easier to refute *for full explanation, see box below*

e.g. The politician's speech burst with emotion as he attacked the opposition leader; but afterwards, his approval rating failed to rise because he had so obviously been **attacking a straw man**, rather than really tackling his chief opponent's arguments

---

A 'straw man' refers to a human-like figure made of straw: one that is easily knocked down, such as a dummy used in military training (the exact origins of the term are unclear).

An example of someone attacking a straw man – instead of the real argument they face – is as follows:

Person X: ice creams are nice
Person Y: but if we only ate ice cream, we'd all develop diabetes and die

In this case, person Y is attacking a straw man by reframing the argument, moving it away from whether or not ice creams are nice (which is a hard thing to disprove as the statement is so subjective), to the easier-to-attack statement that exclusively eating ice creams will lead to health problems.

---

strictures (pl. noun) = **restrictions** (*pronounced 'strik-chers'*) from the Latin, *strictura*, from *stringere*: to draw tight

e.g. Islam's **strictures** – including a ban on alcohol consumption – are well documented

Stygian (adj.) = **very dark** (*pronounced 'stij-ee-uhn'*) *for full explanation, see box below*

e.g. Princess Diana met her end in a car that veered out of control in a **Stygian** tunnel

---

'Stygian' is the adjective denoting 'The Styx', a very dark river in Greek mythology that formed the boundary between earth and the Underworld.

The Greek word behind 'Stygian' is 'stygos', meaning 'hatred'; indeed, the river Styx in ancient Greek mythology was similar to the Christian arena of hatred and suffering, hell. For example, in the poem 'Divine Comedy' by Dante (written in the 14th century), the river Styx is portrayed as a marsh where animosity teems, and where the wrathful and sullen are punished by being drowned in the Styx's murky waters for all eternity.

In keeping with its sinister origins, the adjective 'Stygian' has come to refer to anything that's very dark and dismal.

---

subfusc (adj.) = **dull, gloomy** (*pronounced 'suhb-fuhsk'*) from the Latin, *subfuscus*, from *sub-*: somewhat + *fuscus*: dark brown

e.g. Undertakers generally wear a **subfusc** suit

sub specie aeternitatis (set phrase) = **viewed in comparison to eternity (*i.e. from a detached, universal perspective*)** (*pronounced 'sub spek-ee-ey ay-tern-i-tat-is'*) from the Latin, *sub specie aeternitatis*: under the aspect of eternity

e.g. Unlike animals, humans can rise above their own limited perspective and view their lives **sub specie aeternitatis**; from this giddy height, all human activity can appear without meaning

to sublimate (an unpleasant impulse) into (a pleasant activity) (verb) = **to transform (an unpleasant impulse) into (a pleasant activity)** *(pronounced 'suhb-luh-meyt')* from the Latin, *sublimare*: to elevate, from *sub-*: up to + *limen*: the top of a door; *'sublimation' was a 14th-century phrase used in the medieval practice of alchemy, to refer to 'the process of purifying (a liquid) by heating into a vapour'*

e.g. Lucian Freud was a serious gambler who lost and made millions on the horses; but most of the time, he successfully **sublimated** this addiction to risk **into** making art

to suborn (someone) (verb) = **to induce (someone), via a bribe or via other means, to commit an unlawful act** *(pronounced 'suh-born')* from the Latin, *subornare*: to incite secretly, from *sub-*: secretly + *ornare*: to equip

e.g. When, all of a sudden, the witnesses changed their minds and refused to testify, the judge sensed the mafia had **suborned** them

to subsist on (certain foods or handouts) (verb) = **to support oneself at a minimal level on (certain foods or handouts)** from the Latin, *subsistere*: to stand firm, from *sub-*: from below + *sistere*: to stand

e.g. After he lost all his money in Madoff's investment scam, the old man **subsisted on** buns donated by well-wishers

substantive (adj.) = **important, due to a firm basis in reality** from the Old French, *substantia*: essence

e.g. Some journalists can whip up an article out of thin air, with absolutely nothing **substantive** in the piece at all

succès fou (set phrase) = **a wild success** *(pronounced 'suk-say foo')* from the French, *succès fou*: a wild success

e.g. After noticing that customers kept purchasing cloth to reinforce trousers at exactly the same points of strain (such as at pocket corners), Levi Strauss started using copper rivets to strengthen the pockets of denim work pants: blue jeans have been a **succès fou** ever since

sui generis (adj.) = **constituting a class of its own; unique**
(pronounced 'soo-i ge-ne-ris') from the Latin, *sui generis*: of its own
kind

e.g. You can tell if a painting is a Francis Bacon from a mile off, for
each of his creations was very much **sui generis**

supererogatory (adj.) = *(of a task)* **performed beyond the
required degree** *(pronounced 'soo-per-uh-rog-uh-tawr-ee')* from the
Latin, *supererogare*: to pay in addition, from *super-*: over + *erogare*:
pay out

e.g. He surprised his wife by putting his hands on her shoulders
and administering a **supererogatory** massage

swag (noun) = **an ornamental fabric or garland suspended high
in the air, which hangs down at intervals** from the Old English,
swingan: to swing

e.g. Once you take your seat before a play begins and you look
around you at the **swag** of the darkened theatre, the real world
outside melts away

swain (noun) = **a male lover** *(pronounced 'sweyn')* from the Old
Norse, *sveinn*: lad

e.g. Most fathers are sceptical when their daughters introduce
them to their first **swain**

swingeing (adj.) = **thumpingly large** *(pronounced 'swin-jing')*
from the Old English, *swengan*: to shake

e.g. When you buy a ticket online, budget airlines often hit you
with a **swingeing** debit card charge

sylvan (adj.) = **concerning the woods; pleasantly rural**
(pronounced 'sil-vuhn') from the Latin, *silvanus*: pertaining to the
wood, from *silva*: wood

e.g. Above the fireplace hung a painting of a **sylvan** landscape

Tartarean (adj.) = **hellish** (*pronounced 'tahr-tar-ee-uhn') for full explanation, see box below*

e.g. My aunt was sleeping next door, and all night long I could hear the **Tartarean** depths of her smoker's cough

'Tartarean' is from 'Tartarus', that place in Hades (the underworld in Greek mythology) where the wicked suffered terrible punishment for their crimes on earth.

One of the most famous residents of Tartarus was King Tantalus who languished there as punishment for one particularly terrible act. Desperate to please the gods, Tantalus got a bit carried away preparing a sacrifice to them, and ended up killing his own son, cutting him up and boiling him, before serving him as part of a banquet. But the gods were tipped off about the contents of their forthcoming meal, and avoided Tantalus's gruesome (if fastidiously prepared) feast. Then the whole thing really backfired for Tantalus, when Zeus decided to punish him in a very cruel way.

The exact penalty? Zeus made Tantalus stand in a pool of water beneath a tree with some delicious-looking fruit on its low-lying branches; but whenever Tantalus reached for the fruit, the branches would lift themselves up, raising the fruit just out of his grasp; and, whenever he bent down to get a drink, the water receded before he could get to it in time. The English word 'tantalise' derives from this story (of the suffering of 'Tantalus', one of many tales of woe that took place in 'Tartarus'); whilst the word 'Tartarean' evokes a generally hellish place or state of affairs (like 'Tartarus').

(the) taxonomy of (a group) (noun) = **(the) division into related categories of (a group)** (*pronounced 'tak-son-uh-mee') from the Greek, taxis: arrangement + -nomia: distribution*

e.g. Psychologists seem obsessed with compiling a **taxonomy of** all known human emotions

technocrat (noun) = **a technical specialist who runs a government or a business** (pronounced 'tek-nuh-krat') from the Greek, tekhne: craft + kratos: power

e.g. Now that financial woes have descended on Europe, many governments are being run by staid **technocrats** (rather than by the flamboyant autocrats of the past)

to telegraph (an emotion or thought) = **to non-verbally convey (an emotion or thought)** from the Greek, tele-: at a distance + -graphos: representing, writing

e.g. She said she was looking forward to being divorced, but her pained expression **telegraphed** the concern she was feeling

to temporise (verb) = **to draw out a process in order to gain time** (pronounced 'tem-puh-rise') from the French, temporiser: to bide one's time, from the Latin, temporizare: to delay, ultimately from the Latin, tempus, tempor-: time

e.g. The junior arrived early for the client meeting, and so was forced to **temporise**, asking the client question after question, until finally the boss showed up

tendril (noun) = **a hair-like tentacle** (pronounced 'ten-dril') from the Old French, tendron: a young shoot, from the Latin, tener: tender; a 'tendril' literally means 'a slender appendage of a climbing plant that twines itself around any object in its path'

e.g. Shakespeare wrote a series of plays whose **tendrils** of influence stretch through our language still; for example, our expression 'the green eyed monster' – to describe jealousy – comes from his play The Merchant of Venice

tergiversation (noun) = **the act of turning away from one's opinions** (pronounced 'tur-ji-ver-sey-shun') from the Latin, tergiversari: to turn one's back on, from tergum: back + vertere: to turn

e.g. Politicians are quick to pounce, if their rival comes up with any **tergiversations**, labelling their foe weak for equivocating

tensile (adj.) = **capable of being stretched** (*pronounced 'ten-sahyl'*) from the Latin, *tensilis*, from *tendere*: to stretch

e.g. Bungee-jump rope is composed of hundreds of thick elastic bands renowned for their **tensile** strength

tessellation (noun) = **a pattern consisting of the repetition of one single shape, with no gaps (such as a honeycomb)** (*pronounced 'tes-uh-ley-shuhn'*) from the Latin, *tessellatus*: made up of small square stones, from *tessella*: a small square stone, the diminutive of *tessera*: a square stone

e.g. The floors of office foyers are often composed of marble **tessellations** that make your head spin if you look at their pattern for too long

tetralogy (noun) = **a group of four related literary works** (*pronounced 'te-tral-uh-jee'*) from the Greek, *tetralogia*, from *tetra-*: four + *-logia*: discourse

e.g. Novelist John Updike was most famous for his **tetralogy** covering the life of Harry 'Rabbit' Angstrom: *Rabbit, Run*; *Rabbit Redux*; *Rabbit is Rich*; and *Rabbit at Rest*; Updike said the series was about 'what happens when a young American family man goes on the road – the people left behind get hurt'

Thanatos (noun) = *(in psychology)* **the unconscious urge to die (expressed via an activity such as parachuting and other thrill-seeking sports, for example)** *for full explanation, see box below*

e.g. Christopher Hitchens wrote, 'Dr Martin Luther King...spent his last night on earth in some pretty rough fornication. It's hard to blame him...he lived with the imminence of death and...Eros is the best way yet devised of warding off **Thanatos**'

'Thanatos', which refers to 'the death instinct' in psychology, derives from the Greek, 'thanatos': 'death'. In Greek mythology, 'Thanatos' ('Death') was the son of 'Night' (his mother), and of 'Darkness' (his father). (Incidentally, the names of the other offspring of these two parents read like a litany of dysfunctionality: 'Sleep', twin brother of 'Death'; 'Old Age'; 'Suffering'; 'Doom'; 'Deception'; 'Blame'; 'Strife'; and 'Retribution'. Sunday lunch chez eux doesn't bear thinking about.)

According to Sigmund Freud, humans have two conflicting desires. Firstly, a 'life instinct', which he named 'Eros'. Note that the modern meaning of 'Eros' is 'sexual love', but for Freud, it meant something a bit different: the desire to create and propagate life, via the sating not just of sexual urges but also of hunger and thirst, for example.

'Thanatos', or 'the death instinct' is the conflicting drive to this 'survival instinct' and allegedly compels humans to engage in risky, aggressive and self-destructive acts that could lead to their own death: the desire to pursue thrill-seeking activities like swimming with sharks, for example, is explained by 'Thanatos'.

---

threnody (noun) = **a lament** (*pronounced 'thren-uh-dee'*) from the Greek, *threnos*: wailing + *oilde*: song

e.g. After Princess Diana's death, Elton John rewrote his classic **threnody** *Candle in the Wind* as a tribute to Diana (the song was originally about Marilyn Monroe)

tincture (noun) = **a tiny trace** (*pronounced 'tingk-cher'*) from the Latin, *tinctura*: the act of dyeing, from *tingere*: to dye, tinge; *the sense is of a tiny trace or tint imparted by the process of dyeing (hence 'tincture' means 'a tiny trace')*

e.g. 'Thanks for the good times,' she said, but she failed to disguise the **tincture** of sadness in her voice

to toady to (someone powerful) (set phrase) = **to suck up to (someone powerful)** *for full explanation, see box below*

e.g. She hated going out for corporate dinners with her husband and watching him **toadying to** his rich clients

---

'toady' is a contraction of 'toad-eater', the name in the early 19th century for a charlatan's assistant, whose job it was to eat supposedly poisonous toads. But, of course – unknown to the crowd of onlookers – the toads weren't poisonous at all, so the assistant was fine, not because of the potion he'd publicly imbibed before eating the toads (which the crowd believed had saved him), but because the toads really were harmless. As a result, the deluded crowd bought the potion, hoping it would be a cure-all for them, too.

Since eating a toad is not a pleasant thing to do, these assistants came to epitomise the kind of person who will do anything to get into their boss's good books. Thus, a junior who sucks up to his boss by performing the modern-day equivalent of eating a supposedly poisonous toad (such as perhaps running off, mid-meeting, to get his boss's favourite caramel latte from Starbucks), is still called a 'toady' today.

---

tokenistic (adj.) = *(of an effort)* **going through the motions for the sake of form** *(especially of a workplace that recruits a small number of minorities purely to give the appearance of sexual or racial equality)* from the English words *token* + *-ism*

e.g. Mark Thompson, when head of the BBC, admitted there weren't enough older female newsreaders; yet any effort to address this imbalance appears to be **tokenistic**, for few such newsreaders are on screens still for any broadcaster

torpid (adj.) = **lethargic** from the Latin, *torpidus*, from *torpere*: to be numb

e.g. The day after the wedding, the guests were so hungover that they sat around in a **torpid** state, moaning occasionally

toque (noun) = **a chef's tall white hat** *(pronounced 'tohk')* from the Spanish, *toca*: a woman's headdress

e.g. Old-school cooks don a proper chef's **toque** before preparing a meal

tour de force (set phrase) = **an outstanding display of skill** from the French, *tour de force*: feat of strength

e.g. The critics all agree that *The Great Gatsby* is a literary **tour de force**

tracery (noun) = **a delicate branching pattern** *(pronounced 'trey-suh-ree')* from the Old English, *tracery*: a place for drawing, from the English words, *to trace* + *-ery; Sir Christopher Wren then hijacked the word 'tracery' in the 1660s, using it to refer, in architecture, to intersecting rib work in the upper part of a Gothic window (and from then on in, 'tracery' has evoked a similarly delicate branching pattern)*

e.g. She used to cut her arms with a knife when she was upset; you could still make out a faint **tracery** of scars on her forearm

tract (noun) = **a short piece of writing (on a subject)** *(pronounced 'trakt')* from an abbreviation of the Latin, *tractatus*, from *tractare*: to handle, the frequentative of *trahere*: to draw

e.g. He was so happy to have met his new girlfriend that he wrote a 3,000-word **tract** about their first date

to traduce (someone) (verb) = **to expose (someone) to ridicule** (pronounced 'truh-dyoos') from the Latin, *traducere*: to lead in front of others (and expose to ridicule), from *trans-*: over + *ducere*: to lead

e.g. Obama knew his political opponents would seek to **traduce** him

transcendent (adj.) = **beyond the normal range of human experience** from the Latin, *transcendent-*: climbing over, from *transcendere*: to climb over, from *trans-*: across + *scandere*: to climb

e.g. Militant atheists ridicule anyone claiming **transcendent** experiences

transfigured (adj.) = **made more beautiful** from the Latin, *transfigurare*, from *trans-*: across + *figura*: figure

e.g. After two glasses of wine, the world seems **transfigured**

treatise (noun) = **a lengthy written discourse on a subject**
(*pronounced 'tree-tis'*) from the French, *tretis*, from the Old French,
traitier, from the Latin, *tractare*: to handle, the frequentative of
trahere: to draw

e.g. Academic Noam Chomsky is renowned for his controversial
treatises such as *Media Control: the Spectacular Achievements of
Propaganda*

tremulous (adj.) = **shaking slightly; timid** from the Latin,
tremulus: tremulous, from *tremere*: to tremble + *-ous*

e.g. On her first public appearance as Prince Charles's wife, Diana
gave a **tremulous** smile: she wasn't used to all this attention

to triage (verb) = **to sort a group according to a particular
quality or some other criterion; *for example, in hospitals, 'triage'
refers to the sorting of injured people based on how urgently they
need medical treatment*** from the French, *trier*: to separate out

e.g. She was dating four guys simultaneously but soon, she knew,
she'd have to **triage** them according to suitability for marriage,
and pick just one

triangulation

triangulation (noun) = *(derogatory in tone)* a political policy that cynically adopts the middle ground, so as to neutralise opponents (but also betrays supporters in this way) *for full explanation, see box below*

e.g. Critics of Tony Blair say his decidedly conservative stance on crime and immigration, along with his other **triangulations**, meant he betrayed his party's core principles

---

The word 'triangulation' was coined by Bill Clinton's chief political adviser, Dick Morris, to describe a way of getting Clinton re-elected in the 1996 Presidential election. Morris's crafty plan was for Clinton to present a set of policies that were both 'above' and 'between' the traditional political divisions of 'left' and 'right' (and thus could be said to occupy the top corner of a 'triangle', with 'left' and 'right' making up the other two corners). In this way, any political opponent would be neutralised, because Clinton had adopted for himself at least some of their ideas, thus taking credit for these policies.

So Clinton's adviser Morris had Clinton advocate certain stances – such as 'deregulation' (i.e. lesser government involvement in the way businesses operate) – that were different to traditional Democratic principles and actually closer in tone to the rival Republican Party's goals. Enthusiastically espousing Morris's advice, Clinton famously declared in 1996 that 'the era of big government is over' (a strong hint that 'deregulation' was on the cards). Other politicians worldwide soon adopted Clinton's pursuit of 'triangulations', notably Tony Blair with his 'New Labour' Party.

However, 'triangulation' is now a dirty word, following its failure in the US Presidential election in 2000, when Democrat Al Gore's call for more military spending – traditionally a cry of the Republicans – was seen as an admission that his opponent, George Bush Junior, was correct on this issue. Here, the triangulation backfired. In his book The Audacity of Hope, *Obama seems to allude admiringly to Clinton's 'triangulation' strategy, but cleverly never used the dirty word, referring instead to a 'pragmatic, non-ideological attitude'.*

---

troglodyte (noun) = **an 'out of date' person** *(pronounced 'trog-luh-dahyt')* from the Greek, *troglodytes*: a cave-dweller *(hence a backward person)*

e.g. Some secularists refer to religious people opposed to same-sex marriage as **troglodytes**

trompe l'oeil (set phrase) = **an artwork that deceives the eye**
(*pronounced 'trawmp loi'*) from the French, *trompe l'oeil*: deceives
the eye

e.g. In the art gallery, the visitor made to open the door in front of
him; then he realised this was no door after all, but a **trompe l'oeil**
painted onto the wall

Trotskyist (adj.) = **advocating socialism via a violent revolution**
*(as opposed to being **Fabian** – see earlier – which can refer to the*
achievement of socialism through a more 'softly, softly' approach)
for full explanation, see box below

e.g. When British politician George Gallaway allegedly described
journalist Christopher Hitchens as a 'drink-soaked former
Trotskyist popinjay', Hitchens was said to have responded 'only
some of which is true'

---

*'Trotskyist' literally means 'relating to the economic principles of
Leon Trotsky, especially the theory that socialism should be
established in all countries, explicitly via a revolution'.*

*Leon Trotsky (1879–1940) – along with Vladimir Lenin – was one
of the founders of the Bolshevik Revolution (a key part of the
Russian Revolution of 1917 that removed the Tsars from power)
and, as such, he was one of the few people who had enough
prestige in Russia to be able to challenge the dictatorial rule of
Stalin. So Stalin – a paranoid schizophrenic at the best of times,
who was always worried that people were plotting against him
– made plans to get rid of Trotsky as a potential rival. On 20
August 1940, an assassin sent by Stalin murdered Trotsky by
plunging an ice axe into his head when Trotsky was distracted
reading.*

*Anarchism – the abolition of all organised government – was the
specific path recommended by Trotsky, but the term 'Trotskyist' is
now used as a blanket one, to refer to any form of socialism
achieved violently, by revolution. Incidentally, calling someone a
'Marxist' is nowadays pretty much the same thing as calling them
a 'Trotskyist'; for Karl Marx (the German philosopher who lived
from 1818–83) also advocated a violent revolution, to be carried
out by underprivileged people, in order to topple capitalism.
(Finally, 'popinjay' – the end of the insult levelled at Hitchens in
the example above – means 'a vain talker', and was originally the
Middle English word for that great talker of a bird, the parrot.)*

trove (noun) = **a store of valuable objects** from the English expression, *treasure trove*, which comes from the French, *tresor trouvé:* found treasure

e.g. The US military was heartened at their discovery of a **trove** of al-Qaeda documents near the Syrian border

tub-thumping (adj.) = *(derogatory in tone)* **ranting** from the English word, *tub*, the 17th-century slang for *pulpit; hence 'tub-thumper' (1662) meant 'a speaker who thumps the pulpit by way of emphasis'*

e.g. Kim Jong Il gave another **tub-thumping** speech, which was greeted with yet more applause

to be riding the tumbrel to the guillotine (set phrase) = **to be on your way out** *(literally: to be in the open cart – or 'tumbrel' – used to transport aristocrats to the guillotine in the French Revolution, 1789 –99)* from the Old French, *tomberel*: tumbrel, from *tomber*: to fall (*for the cart's contents – the artistocrats about to be beheaded – would unceremoniously fall over when the cart was tipped to the ground in front of the guillotine)*

e.g. In his final years, the Alzheimers-striken Ronald Reagan looked tired and anguished, like a man **riding the tumbrel to the guillotine**

tundra (noun) = **a wasteland** from the Lappish, *tundar*: elevated wasteland; *the 'tundra' is a desolate region around the North Pole, where the subsoil is frozen, meaning no trees can grow*

e.g. When he got the email saying his divorce was final, he suddenly felt cut off from all humanity, as if alone on a **tundra**

turbid (adj.) = *(of a liquid)* **cloudy, disturbed** *(pronounced 'tur-bid')* from the Latin, *turbidus*, from *turba*: a crowd, a disturbance

e.g. The depressed man surveyed for a moment the **turbid** Thames below, then jumped

tyke (noun) = **a small child** *(pronounced 'tike')* from the Old English, *tyke*: mongrel, from the Old Norse, *tik*: bitch

e.g. My plane journey was terrible because I was sat next to a mother with a screaming **tyke** on her knee

tyro (noun) = **a novice** *(pronounced 'tiro')* from the Latin, *tiro*: a novice soldier

e.g. With publishers preferring writers who are already celebrities, it's increasingly tough for the **tyro** novelist to get a break

U

umami (noun) = **the meaty taste of mushrooms and the like** *(considered to be the fifth taste, along with sweet, sour, salty and bitter)* *(pronounced 'oo-mah-mee')* from the Japanese, *umami*: deliciousness

e.g. The taste of miso soup – which is quite meaty, without actually being meat – is what is meant by **umami**

umbrageous (adj.) = **easily offended** *(pronounced 'uhm-bre-juhs')* from the Latin, *umbra*: shadow; *over time, the figurative use of 'umbrage' to mean 'displeasure' evolved from the connection between physical darkness (due to shadows) and mental gloominess of thought (but 'umbrageous' can still be used in its literal sense of physically 'shadowy' today)*

e.g. He used to be such a convivial chap; but after his wife died, he became **umbrageous**, and most conversations with him ended in an argument

unalloyed (adj.) = *(of an emotion)* **pure;** *the word literally refers to a metal that is not in a mixture or alloy (i.e. 'unalloyed') with other metals, and, hence, 'pure'* *(pronounced 'un-al-oi-ed')* the negative of the French, *aloier*: to combine, from the Latin, *alligare*: to bind

e.g. As Kate Middleton walked down the aisle, her expression was one of **unalloyed** joy

undulating (adj.) = **having a wavy form** from the Latin, *undulatus*: like a wave, from *unda*: a wave

e.g. For Oscar night, actresses seem fond of wearing their hair in **undulating** curls

unguent (noun) = **a soft greasy substance used as ointment** *(pronounced 'un-gwunt')* from the Latin, *unguentum*: ointment, from *unguere*: to anoint with ointment

e.g. Pharmaceutical companies cynically promote their latest **unguent** as a miracle cure for bad skin

unimpeachable (adj.) = *(of a person) of the highest possible repute (literally: 'not allowed to be questioned, or impeached')* from the Old French, *empêcher*: to impede, from the Latin, *impedicare*: to entangle, based on *pedica*: a fetter, from *pes, ped-*: foot

e.g. His wife dismissed the rumours of her husband's infidelity; for, in her eyes, he was **unimpeachable**

unprepossessing (adj.) = **not very attractive** from the English words, *un* + *to prepossess*: to impress favourably; *'to prepossess' means 'to possess mentally beforehand, like an act of prejudice' – but the prejudice (or 'prejudging') implied here is a positive one , so, 'to prepossess' means 'to impress favourably from the outset'*

e.g. The sex appeal of politicians lies not in their often **unprepossessing** appearances, but in the power that they wield

unspool (verb) = *(of a memory or of a real-time event)* to unwind, as if from a film spool** from the English words, *un* + *spool*: a cylindrical device around which something is wound (itself from the French, *espole*: a spool)

e.g. As Federer and Nadal finally arrived on court, everyone wondered how the Wimbledon final would **unspool**

untrammelled by (something) (adj.) = **unrestricted by (something)** from the Old English, *trammel*: net to catch a fish, ultimately from the Latin, *tremaculum*: a net made from three layers of meshes, from *tri-*: three + *macula*: mesh

e.g. Shakespeare rose above his peers because he had a mind **untrammelled by** convention

unvarnished (adj.) = *(of a statement)* **unembellished** the negative of the French, *vernis*: varnish, from the medieval Latin, *veronix*: fragrant resin

e.g. The late Ginger McCain, an outspoken racehorse trainer, was fond of giving **unvarnished** opinions such as: 'Horses do not win Nationals when ridden by women'

(sunlit) uplands

(sunlit) uplands (set phrase) = **the promised land** from the
English words *sunlit* + *upland*: an area of high land

e.g. Perhaps one day this current economic gloom will lift, to
reveal **sunlit uplands** once more

ur- *(placed in front of a noun)* = **earliest** from the German, *ur-*:
original

e.g. As a reaction against her **ur-**feminist of a mother, who was
always absent pursuing her career, she decided to devote herself
exclusively to child-raising

valence (noun) = **the capacity of one person (or thing) to affect another in some special way** *(pronounced 'vey-luhns')* from the Latin, *valentia*: strength

e.g. On a first date, both parties are influenced – without realising it – by the **valences** of the other person's smell

valetudinarian (adj.) = **a sickly person who is justifiably concerned with their health; OR** *(ironic in tone)* **a person who is in fact healthy and is needlessly concerned with their health** from the Latin, *valetudinarius*: in ill health, from *valetudo*: health, from *valere*: to be well

e.g. When his Navy patrol boat was sunk in World War II, JFK suffered terrible injuries that rendered him a lifelong **valetudinarian**

to vamp for (someone) (verb) = **to improvise for someone's benefit** *'to vamp' literally means 'to improvise a musical accompaniment in jazz'*

e.g. If a guest is struggling to answer his questions, a TV interviewer will start **vamping for** that guest in an attempt to take the conversation off on a new tangent

vassal (adj.) = *(of a person or of a whole nation)* **in a subordinate position to another** *(because the vassal has declared fealty to the other, see the entry for fealty earlier)* *(pronounced 'vas-uhl')* from the medieval Latin, *vassallus*: retainer

e.g. Some journalists say the United States regards the United Kingdom as no more than a **vassal** state that will come running when called

vastation (noun) = **a laying waste** from the Latin, *vastatio*: vastation, from *vastare*: to lay waste

e.g. Auschwitz was a **vastation** that shook up the world

venturesome

venturesome (adj.) = **willing to take on risks or dangers** from the English words *venture* + *-some*

e.g. Bruce Lee's home was once broken into by a **venturesome** individual who was intent on making a name for himself by confronting Lee; but just one kick from the martial arts guru was enough to incapacitate the intruder

to veer between the Scylla of *(one danger)* and the Charybdis of *(a second danger)* (set phrase) = to attempt to circumnavigate two equally terrifying dangers (knowing that, if you steer clear of one, you are putting yourself in the path of the other) *('Scylla' is pronounced 'sil-uh'; and 'Charybdis' as 'Kuh-rib-dis') for full explanation, see box below*

e.g. To beat Roger Federer, you have to not only **veer between the Scylla of** his forehand and **the Charybdis of** his backhand; but also to then remember to hit a winner yourself

---

'Scylla' and 'Charybdis' were two terrifying monsters in Ancient Greek mythology. They lived opposite each other, with just a narrow channel of water separating them: thus, they posed a huge risk to sailors, who had to attempt to veer an even course between these two horrors. For Scylla had six heads – each equipped with three rows of razor-sharp teeth – and a cat's tail; whilst Charybdis was one giant bladder of a creature, whose face was all mouth and whose arms and legs were tiny flippers. (Charybdis was built this way because three times a day she'd swallow a huge amount of water before belching it back out again, so as to create dangerous whirlpools to sink passing ships with.)

Both monsters started life as beautiful women, but then fell foul of the gods, who transformed them into beasts. In the case of Scylla, she was originally a gorgeous nymph, but then the goddess Circe (Scylla's love rival) poured poison into the pool where Scylla bathed, turning Scylla into a six-headed monster. From then on, whenever the embittered Scylla spied a ship, each of her six heads would seize one of the crew and devour them alive. As for Charybdis, it was Zeus, king of the gods, who turned this one-time beauty into an unsightly monster. Her crime? Well, Charybdis began life as daughter of the sea god Poseidon, and fought alongside her father in his endless feud against Zeus (Charybdis's signature move was to wait for her father to stir up an ocean storm, then drive the resulting waves onto land, swamping whole villages and claiming them for the sea. No wonder Zeus had it in for her.)

In Homer's epic poem the Odyssey *(c. 800 BC), the hero Odysseus attempted to steer his ship on a perfectly even course, right down the middle of these two monsters, thus avoiding them both. But so keen was he to avoid Charybdis – whom Odysseus considered the more dangerous since her whirlpools could submerge his entire ship – that Odysseus ended up sailing too close to Scylla, who promptly grabbed six of his men and ate them whole. Traditionally, the two monsters have been associated with a real place: the Strait of Messina off the coast of Sicily, where a vortex – identified with Charybdis – is caused by the meeting of currents, whilst the rock opposite on the Italian mainland is identified with Scylla. Regardless of whether this place gave birth to the myth or not, the phrase 'veering between Scylla and Charybdis' continues to mean 'steering between two great dangers' today.*

verisimilitude (noun) = **the appearance of reality** *(pronounced 'ver-uh-si-mil-it-yood')* from the Latin, *verisimilitudo*, from *verisimilis*: probable, from *veri*: genitive of *verus*: true + *simile*: like

e.g. The dialogue in the TV series *Gavin and Stacey* was bursting with **verisimilitude**, right down to some characters talking over other characters who were mid-speech at the time of interruption: an unusually true-to-life technique for TV dialogue

vernal (adj.) = **to do with spring** (pronounced 'vur-nul') from the Latin, *vernalis*: of the spring, from *ver*: spring

e.g. Spring imparts a **vernal** optimism

vestigial (adj.) = *(of a remnant)* **tiny, but once part of something bigger** *(pronounced 've-stij-uhl')* from the Latin, *vestigium*: a footprint

e.g. Even now, ten years after the divorce, he still felt a **vestigial** flicker of anger whenever his ex-wife's name was mentioned

virago

virago (noun) = **a domineering, irritable woman** (*pronounced 'vi-<u>rah</u>-go'*) from the Latin, *vir*: man + *-ago* (a suffix that re-genders the word to be female) *for full explanation, see box below*

e.g. To her female supporters, suffragette Emily Davison – who died when she threw herself under the King's horse in the 1913 Epson Derby (as an act of protest on behalf of women) – was a heroine; to her male detractors, she was a shrieking **virago**

Greek philosophers, who believed women were inferior to men, did concede that certain women surpassed the expectations for what was believed possible for their gender, and even reached masculine-like excellence. Such a woman was called a 'virago', deriving from the Latin 'vir': 'a man'. Originally, then, 'virago' was a title of respect and admiration.

In history, there are many recorded instances of women who earned the title 'virago' (in this positive sense) – Joan of Arc is a famous example – often when carrying out a traditionally masculine role, such as fighting battles, wearing men's clothing or sporting the haircut of a male monk (a tonsure).

But these 'viragos' caused social anxiety for a certain kind of insecure male, who saw strong women as a threat. So the word 'virago' was hijacked and started to be used disparagingly, to imply that a woman who was a 'virago', far from being heroic, was in fact overbearing. Thus 'virago' joined the long list of pejoratives – such as 'termagant' and 'shrew' – which men have invented to demean strong women (though women have been much more gracious, and invented very few such equivalent terms to put down men).

(a) votary of (a person or group) (noun) = **a devoted follower of (a person or group)** (*pronounced '<u>voh</u>-tuh-ree'*) from the Latin, *votum*: a vow; *a 'votary' is literally a person who is bound by vows of a religious nature, such as a monk or a nun*

e.g. The young Charles M. Schulz, creator of *Peanuts*, had his drawings rejected by the high school yearbook; but 60 years later – much to the delight of Schulz's many **votaries** – a five-foot-tall statue of Snoopy was placed in the school's main office

(a) votive offering (set phrase) = **an offering made in fulfilment of a vow** *('votive' is pronounced 'voh-tiv')* from the Latin, *votivus*: relating to a vow, ultimately from *votum*: a vow

e.g. *Pan's Labyrinth* director Guillermo del Toro, when in his twenties, published a 500-page book about Alfred Hitchcock, which del Toro has called 'a **votive offering** to a god beyond reach'

to vouchsafe (someone) (something) (verb) = **to give (something) (to someone) in a gracious or condescending way** from the Old English, *vouchen safe*: to vouch as safe

e.g. Religious people see any good fortune in their lives as a blessing **vouchsafed** them by heaven

vox populi / vox pop (noun) = **the opinions of the majority** *('vox populi' is pronounced 'voks pop-yuh-lahy')* from the Latin, *vox populi*: the voice of the people

e.g. Horizontal stripes actually make you look thinner, not fatter: a fact that fashionistas have officially established in various **vox pop** polls

vulgarian (noun) = **a person who is considered unrefined, especially one who has only recently acquired influence or money** *(pronounced 'vuhl-gair-ee-uhn')* from the Latin, *vulgaris*, from *vulgus*: common people

e.g. Coco Chanel was much taken by the bevelled edges of her lover's whisky decanter: here, thought Coco, is a look that will be embraced by the chic and shunned by **vulgarians**, and, on the spot, she invented her iconic perfume bottle

waggish (adj.) = **humorous in a mischievous manner** *for full explanation, see box below*

e.g. When he was diagnosed with prostate cancer, legendary investor Warren Buffet played down the news, **waggishly** stating of the disease and his chances of mortality, '... maybe I'll get shot by a jealous husband, but this is a really minor thing'

From the Old English, 'waghalter': 'gallows bird'; this referred to someone who was destined to swing in a noose (a 'halter' in Old English), and was – rather alarmingly – used mainly of mischievous children, with the droll implication being that such miscreants deserved the gallows.

---

wallah (noun) = **a person concerned or involved with a specific thing or business** (*pronounced 'wah-la'*) from the Hindi suffix, *-vala*: doer, from the Sanskrit, *palaka*: keeper

e.g. It was shortly after the CEO requested his secretary wear shorter skirts that he got a phone call from the HR **wallah**

(the) warp and weft of (something) (set phrase) = **(the) tapestry of (something)** *for full explanation, see box below*

e.g. Squabbles and subsequent reconciliations are all part of **the warp and weft of** family life

---

'the warp and weft' are key terms in weaving; 'the weft' refers to all those crosswise threads on a loom, over and under which the other threads – collectively known as 'the warp' – are passed.

---

weathervane (noun) = *(of a person)* **someone who changes his mind in line with the masses** *the word 'weathervane' literally refers to a revolving pointer mounted on top of a building to show the direction of the wind: consequently, a 'weathervane' swings around a lot*

e.g. A politician who frequently changes his mind – in an attempt to capture the public's mood at any one point – will quickly be labelled a **weathervane** by his rivals

weevil (noun) = *(of a person)* **someone who gets into your head** *(pronounced 'wee-vuhl') a 'weevil' is literally a small beetle with a long snout, which lays larvae that then develop inside plant stems, damaging them*

e.g. Since they used to be such good friends, Karl Jung took Sigmund Freud's later criticisms of him very much to heart: for Jung, it was as if a **weevil** had burrowed into his soul

whey-faced (adj.) = *(of a person)* **pale, usually owing to disease or shock** *(pronounced 'way-faced') from the English word, whey: the watery part of milk that remains after the rest of the milk has turned into cheese (when you leave milk for a long time)*

e.g. For many people, the word 'student' conjures up the image of a **whey-faced** youth in a bedsit

whirligig (noun) = *(of a thing)* **frantic and constantly changing** *(pronounced 'wur-li-gig') from the Middle English, to whirl + gig: a top; a 'whirligig' literally means 'a toy that spins around, such as a top'*

e.g. People obsessed with status symbols are trapped in a **whirligig** of envy

whorl (noun) = **a twisted spiral** *(pronounced 'wurl') from the Middle English, to whirl, influenced by the Old English, wharve: the whorl of a spindle*

e.g. A new mother can admire something as simple as the **whorl** of her baby's ear for hours on end

wildcat (adj.) = **not authorised by the proper authorities, not officially endorsed** *from the English words, wild + cat; the first sense, in the 16th century, was of 'a savage woman'; by the 19th century, this had morphed to mean 'one who peddles rash projects', before changing further into today's meaning*

e.g. A caricature of the Prophet Mohammed, printed on the front page of a Norwegian tabloid, sparked **wildcat** strikes by Muslim taxi drivers in Oslo in 2010

wiseacre

wiseacre (noun) = **a know-it-all** *(pronounced 'wise-ey-ker')* from the Middle Dutch, *wijsseggher*: soothsayer, from the Germanic bases of *wit* and *say*; *no one has any idea how the word 'acre' crept into the English expression*

e.g. The worst thing you can do in politics is to consider things from your opponents' point of view – or so say the **wiseacres**

wonkish (adj.) = *(derogatory in tone)* **a studious person who takes an excessive interest in minor details** *'a wonk' came about from the shortening of the British slang 'wanker' (presumably since a 'wanker' is a slang way of referring to a 'know-it-all', which is what a 'wonk' is – albeit a 'know-it-all' within a narrow field)*

e.g. Fans of Barack Obama say that he is a man of the people whereas his rival politicians are focused on **wonkish** matters that most people don't care about

wraith (noun) = **a person who is so thin they look insubstantial, like a ghost** *(pronounced 'reyth') a 'wraith' literally means 'a ghost or a ghostlike image of a person, usually seen shortly before or after they die' as per Scottish beliefs in the 16th century*

e.g. In the strip club, starved Eastern European girls in G-strings were twisting around the poles like **wraiths**

Xanadu (noun) = **a place so luxurious or beautiful, that it is almost unattainably so** (pronounced '<u>zan</u>-uh-doo') for full explanation, see box below

e.g. Coco Chanel regarded the Ritz, Paris as her own **Xanadu**: she lived there for 30 years and died there in 1971

'Xanadu' was the name of the beautiful city where Kublai Khan (1215–94), Emperor of China (and grandson of Genghis Khan), spent his summers. Located in what is now called Inner Mongolia, about 350 km north of present-day Beijing, Xanadu (built between 1252 and 1256) was a most striking place, which had 100,000 people living inside it at its peak. Venetian explorer Marco Polo – who visited the city in 1275 – described it thus: 'a very fine marble Palace, the rooms of which are all gilt and painted with figures of men and beasts and birds, and with a variety of trees and flowers, all executed with such exquisite art that you regard them with delight and astonishment. Round this Palace a wall is built, enclosing a compass of 16 miles, and inside the Park there are fountains and rivers and brooks, and beautiful meadows, with all kinds of wild animals (excluding such as are of ferocious nature), which the Emperor has procured and placed there to supply food for his gerfalcons and hawks, which he keeps there in mew.'

But it was the poet Samuel Coleridge who immortalised the city in his poem 'Kubla Khan' (1797); Coleridge wrote the poem after reading a rival historical account of the city, smoking a lot of opium, then falling asleep and having a vision of the place. The poem starts thus,

'In Xanadu did Kubla Khan
A stately pleasure-dome decree:
Where Alph, the sacred river, ran
Through caverns measureless to man
Down to a sunless sea.'

As a result of these melodious words, 'Xanadu' became a byword for luxury and has been referenced in numerous ways since: 'Xanadu', for example, was the name of Charles Foster Kane's estate in the film Citizen Kane; and in an episode of Seinfeld, Jerry refers to George's bathroom, with its view of the Manhattan skyline and private bar, as 'Xanadu'.

to have a yen for (something) / to do (something)

(set phrase) = **to have a longing for (something) / to do (something)** from the Chinese, *yan*: the craving of a drug addict for a drug

e.g. Sensing his death was imminent, writer John Steinbeck **had a yen to** travel across the United States one last time; this he did, in the company of his faithful poodle Charley, and the result was his final book *Travels with Charley*

Zelig-like (adj.) = *(of a person)* attending many of the most significant occasions of the 20th century; OR able to change their appearance or attitude, so as to be at ease in any situation (*'zelig' is pronounced 'zel-ig') for full explanation, see box below*

e.g. US President Ronald Reagan was thrown, **Zelig-like**, into some key events of the 20th century, such as the USA's 1986 bombing of Libya and the ending of the Cold War

or

e.g. Within a couple of hours of being introduced to the parents of her boyfriend, she was subconsciously copying some of their facial gestures, **Zelig-like** as she was

---

'Zelig-like' derives from the name of Leonard Zelig, the protagonist in Woody Allen's film Zelig (1983). Zelig is a chameleon of a man, who has such a strong desire to fit in and be liked that he automatically takes on the traits of any personality in his vicinity.

In the film, when the media takes an interest in a psychiatrist's attempts to cure him, Zelig becomes world famous. He starts to associate with fellow celebrities from the 20th century, like Al Capone and F. Scott Fitzgerald (with Woody Allen's technical wizardry allowing Zelig to appear to stand alongside these figures on screen).

Nowadays, 'Zelig-like' refers to either a person who is as chameleonic as the fictional Leonard Zelig is (such as the use of 'Zelig-like' in this sentence, 'He was happy to dispense advice to both the Democrats and the Republicans since he was Zelig-like in his own political affiliations'); or else, 'Zelig-like' simply refers to a person who was as ubiquitous as Zelig was (in the film), where he hobnobs with virtually all of the stars of – and attends many of the main events of – the 20th century.

---

zephyr (noun) = **a very light piece of clothing** (*pronounced 'zef-er') from the Greek, zephuros: (god of) the west wind; a 'zephyr' can also mean in English 'a soft gentle breeze'*

e.g. The name 'Coco Chanel' summons up a **zephyr**-clad nymph; but, in fact, the fashionista was allegedly a Nazi collaborator

zeugma (noun) = a figure of speech where a word applies to two other words but in different ways (e.g. 'Gwendoline and her passport expired last week'); or to two words when it only really semantically suits one of these two (e.g. 'with wailing mouths and hearts') *(pronounced 'zug-ma')* from the Greek, *zeugnunai*: to yoke, related to *zugon*: yoke

e.g. The singer Alanis Morissette seems to be a fan of **zeugma**, as evidenced by her lyrics, 'You held your breath and the door for me'

Zionist (adj.) = *(of a person)* supporting a Jewish national state in Israel *(pronounced 'zahy-uh-nizt') for full explanation, see box below*

e.g. There has been universal condemnation of those conspiracy theorists who insist that 9/11 was a **Zionist** plot, designed to provoke the United States into attacking Israel's enemies

According to Judaism, Israel is a land promised to the Jews by God (as set down in the Bible); and 'Zion' – referred to in the Bible by the Hebrew word 'Tsiyon' – is a hill in Jerusalem that has long stood as a symbol for this Land of Israel. (Hence one who is pro-Zion, or a 'Zionist', is pro- not just the hill, but also the concept of Israel.)

After several instances of anti-semitic persecution around 1900 – including the pogroms in Russia – Jewish scholars advocated the return of Jews to their historical homeland of Israel, a process that culminated in the establishment of the state of Israel in 1948. Today, almost half of all Jews worldwide reside in Israel.

Critics of Zionism say that it is a racist movement, as it promotes segregation on the grounds of race (i.e. apartheid). In fact, the UN passed a resolution in 1975 officially deeming Zionism 'a form of racism' (this resolution was repealed in 1991). Many in the Middle East see the Israelis as foreign aggressors, pointing out that there was no Israel 100 years ago, and claiming that the land now known as Israel in fact belongs to the Palestinian Arabs (who were forcibly displaced to make way for the newcomers). In addition, many countries – notably Iran – regard Israel as Muslim territory that must be repatriated. On the other hand, though, Israelis claim that anti-Zionism is just anti-semitism dressed up in a different way.

Sources

Cawthorne, Nigel. *Sex Lives of Hollywood Idols*. London: Prion Books, 2004.

Dillon-Malone, Aubrey. *Funny Peculiar: A Directory of the Daft and Dotty*. London: Prion Books, 1991.

Parish, James Robert. *The Hollywood Book of Death*. New York: McGraw-Hill, 2001.

Schnakenberg, Robert. *Secret Lives of Great Authors*. Philadelphia: Quirk Books, 2008.

Soanes, Catherine and Angus Stevenson. *Oxford Dictionary of English*. Oxford: Oxford University Presss, 2005.

Online Etymology Dictionary: www.etymonline.com

www.wikipedia.org

Acknowledgements

A big 'thank you' to: Sheila Ableman, my friend and agent; Kathy Rooney, Alana Clogan, Sophia Blackwell and the team at Bloomsbury; Sandra Howgate for her delightfully quirky drawings; Colin Dexter for his kind quote; Louisa for inspiring me and for editing; Robin for 'objective correlative'; Crispin and Nichola for great advice, and Crispin for 'acedia', 'isomorphic' and 'obloquy'; and to Dom, Alex, Jasper, Digger Louisa, Feras, Piers, John, Paul, Harry, Amanda, Nigel, Michael H., Lady Murton, my wonderful 10 siblings and Rosemary for all their support.

Acknowledgements

Also a special expression of gratitude to the readers of The Daily Telegraph, *who so generously drew my attention to their favourite words: Gaetana Trippetti (for 'Lucullan'); Eva Amann (for 'Mephistophelean'); C. Willgoose (for 'cynosure' and many others); Klara Banaszak (for 'swingeing'); Mike Roberts (for 'threnody'); Professor John Drearden (for too many to list here); Marc Gonsalves (for 'pastiche'); Victoria Godfrey (for 'valetudinarian'); Patricia Law (for reams of useful words); David Bissell (for 'periphrasis'); Jack McCoull (for 'adumbrate'); Bonnie Shortt (for 'subfusc'); Harry Smith, as well as Sandra Noble (both – independently – for 'supererogation'); Barbara Thatcher (for 'basilisk'); Sue Lessels, as well as Robert Hunt, Tony Darrah and Mike Wicking (all for pointing out – independently – the true etymology of 'sesquipedalian'); Vicky Liddell (for 'Stygian'); Des Taylor (for 'animadversion'); Chris Brooker (for so many that there's no room to list them); Mike Humphries (for 'virago'); William Alexander (for 'abnegate'); Derek Aldred (for 'plosive'); Sheila Williams (for 'defenestrate'); Reg Vallintine, as well as Bill Hudson (both – independently – for 'concupiscent'); Terry Walker (for 'lubricious'); Gavin Inglis (for 'persiflage'); Mickie Wynne-Davies, John Maskell and Ann Spencer (all – independently – for 'verisimilitude'); Madeleine Thomas (for 'gonzo'); John Conway (for 'exegesis'); Tamara Shanks (for 'sinecure'); Peter Bird, as well as V. Phillips (both – independently – for 'divagating'); Brian Gould, as well as John Southern (both – independently – for 'eleemosynary'); Richard Munday (for 'pabulum'); Doug Sollars (for 'troglodyte'); Simon Bryden-Brook (for 'nugatory'); Roger Marjoribanks (for 'pullulating'); Diggory Seacombe (for 'zeugma'); and all other readers for their kind suggestions.*

Please contact me with views, criticisms and all else at: hubert_vandenbergh@yahoo.co.uk